The Cat's Pajamas

The Cat's Pajamas

A Fabulous Fictionary of Familiar Phrases

TAD TULEJA

FAWCETT COLUMBINE · NEW YORK

A Fawcett Columbine Book
Published by Ballantine Books
Copyright © 1987 by Thaddeus F. Tuleja

Grateful acknowledgment is made to Dover Publications, Inc. for
permission to print seventeen illustrations from *Humorous Victorian Spot
Illustrations*, edited by Carol Belanger Grafton, 1985.

Library of Congress Catalog Card Number: 87-91557

ISBN: 0-449-90242-0

Cover design by Dale Fiorillo
Book design by Beth Tondreau Design
Manufactured in the United States of America

First Edition: January 1988
10   9   8   7   6   5   4

For Andrée

la migliore fabbra

Lucat bene si ergo
Fortibus es inero
O nobili demis trux
Sum et causen summit dux

—Anon.

Introduction

*I*dioms and figures of speech are the DARK HORSES of our language: They add color and spice to the proceedings, but nobody seems to know where they came from.

A few examples: Everybody knows that to be absolutely happy is to be HAPPY AS A CLAM. But who was the genius who first imagined bivalves with emotions? Who in the distant shadows of history made the ornithologically inaccurate but metaphorically deathless observation that crows always fly a straight line? We know what it means to have the *wool pulled over our eyes*, but what arcane practice gave rise to the expression? Why is it CAT'S PAJAMAS, of all things, and not dog's, or clam's, or crow's, or dark horse's pajamas? And why on earth does DONE TO A T mean anything to us at all?

It was to solve such mysteries that I wrote *The Cat's Pajamas*. Composed in fugitive moments of beetle-browed whimsy, and driven by the same intellectual curiosity that lies behind every great leap of the civilized mind, it provides what I believe to be plausible explanations—at least as "meaningful" as the idioms themselves—for the origins of today's popular expressions, from UP IN THE AIR to CATCHING ZS.

I began the research for this volume rather casually, still unsure, scientifically speaking, if such a book were really needed. Very quickly, however, I discovered a number of shocking lacunae in the explanations from the Standard Authorities on Language. Puzzling over why PULLING ONE'S LEG, for example, should be a metaphor for duping or teasing, I consulted William Safire and H. L. Mencken and the British slang expert Eric Partridge and even the sacred *Oxford English Dictionary*. The best that I could come up with was Partridge's hint that "pulling" might stand here for "tripping," and the phrase indicate a practical joke.

That was much too flimsy to be satisfying, so, putting aside my reverence for St. Eric, I constructed a less mundane explanation of my own. As with all ground-breaking mental labor, the exercise proved both enjoyable and, in an offbeat way, illuminating. Fired with the novelty, I did the same thing for HAPPY AS A CLAM, and CHEWING THE FAT, and TONGUE IN CHEEK until I had the less than one billion entries contained here.

In putting these entries together, I tried to keep an agreeable tableau in mind. I imagined myself at a dinner party seated between the American lexicographer Noah Webster and the Argentinian fantasist Jorge Luis Borges. If I were lucky enough to engage those two very different word-fanciers in a conversation about figures of speech, I asked myself, what riches would be revealed?

The answer was clear. Mixing the straightforward etymologies of Mr. Webster with the crazy-quilt constructs of Sr. Borges would yield an amalgam of the bona fide and the bizarre. The result would be the stuff of language itself: a richly satisfying tension between the sane, sober learning of New England and the pixilated erudition of Buenos Aires—between fact and what fancy would make of it. This "fictionary" was born of that tension.

Of course, if you already know the story of Alasdair Slyke's brush with death that gave us PULLING ONE'S LEG; if you're already familiar with the Eskimo mating ritual that produced the phrase

CHEWING THE FAT; if you already know the details of how Eduardo Zabaglione gave his name to EASY STREET—then this book will not help you at all.

If you don't know those details, however, then there's a good chance that it will. Likewise if you're foggy on the origin of FOGGY-MINDED (see page 88: It has nothing to do with the weather), or of FLY BY NIGHT (page 86; nothing to do with airplanes), or of *Nose In the Air* (page 197; no hints here about *that* one). Ditto if you're not sure why we call BOOZE (page 32) "booze" (and vice versa). And if you still believe that old story about HIS NAME IS MUD (page 50) being connected to John Wilkes Booth's bonesetter—well, then, you can hardly afford *not* to read on.

Now, I know a lot of folks don't GIVE A DAMN (page 64). They're perfectly content to go on using the expressions explained here without knowing what they're saying between the lines. If you're one of those self-satisfied folks, fine. It's well recognized that IGNORANCE IS BLISS (see Sam Bliss's story, page 123); who am I to disturb your slumber? If you don't mind going through life LAUGHING UP YOUR SLEEVE (page 138) at linguists without appreciating the pornographic implications of your actions, that's all right with me. Just don't CRY IN YOUR BEER (page 63) when you go to that really important board meeting or cocktail party and somebody quotes from this book and you look like the only RUBE (page 181) there.

I'm betting you're not another rube. I'm betting you care about your language. You read Safire; you play the Dictionary Game; you do the *Times* crossword in pen. Your home has a Wilson Follett shrine. You're quadrilingual, am I right? This book was written for you. Take it as an exercise, if you will, in what the Germans might call *Augenblitzenlexikographie*, or "dictionary-making with a twinkle in the eye."

Among those to whom I am indebted for keeping a twinkle in my eye are Voltaire, who quipped that history is "but the story we agree upon"; Oscar Wilde, who observed in *The Importance of Being Earnest* that "It is a terrible thing for a man to find out suddenly that all his life he has been speaking nothing but the truth"; and all those genial librarians, from Buenos Aires to Cold Springs Plantation, who pointed me to fodder for this canon.

File it, fellow bookworms, under Fakelore.

T.T.
Cold Springs
April 1, 1987

NOTE: Cross references to other entries appear in small capitals and may be found by referring to the index. Variant forms, which are also indexed, appear in italic in the main entries.

The
Cat's
Pajamas

Up in the Air

Among the more frivolous amusements popular in the court of France's Sun King, Louis XIV, was an indoor sport known as "*Bout de Souffle*," or "Out of Breath." Courtiers would gather in the grand ballroom at Versailles, where each would be given a small feather. At the signal to begin, the feathers would be hurled into the air, and the courtiers would attempt to keep them aloft using only their breath. This provided much amusement to the court, not only because of the inevitable clatter of bodies, but also because, after a minute or two of sustained puffing, virtually all the players would be panting and lightheaded, and not a few would fall down unconscious. The game could end, and a winner be declared, only after all but one feather had fallen to the ground; until that point, the proceedings were said, literally enough, to be still *en l'air,* or *up in the air*; hence the idiom for anything still undecided.

To aficionados of French films it will be obvious that the movie which made Jean-Paul Belmondo a star, *Bout de Souffle* (*Breathless*), took its title, as a kind of Gallic insider's joke, from the game. What may not be so obvious is that the supposedly Californian expression *airhead*, meaning someone without discernible intelligence, also refers to Bout de Souffle. The etymological route from seventeenth-century France to twentieth-century Los Angeles is too circuitous to follow here. Suffice it to say that the original airheads were dizzy, winded French courtiers. To be giddy or foolish-looking in Louis's France was to have, like them, a *tête à l'air.* (The details of the French–Californian connection may be found in Abba Duse's charming *History of Stupidity*.)

Putting on Airs

The original of this phrase was "putting on bronze." Carrying the same sense of pretension as the modern version, it referred to the ancient Phrygian custom of wearing bronze coins, usually on necklaces, as a sign of status. The Romans, who learned of this practice in the first century B.C., considered it barbarically ostentatious, and they began to speak of pretentious persons in general as being, like the Phrygians, *aere ornati*, or "decked in bronze." English-speaking people encountered the idea in late medieval translations of Ovid and Livy, but they encountered it in a mistranslation. We might today still speak of a conceited person as "putting on bronze" were it not for the closeness of Latin *aer*, meaning bronze, and *āēr*, meaning air. Evidently it was a poor Latin scholar, ignorant of the difference in vowel lengths, who translated *aere ornati* as "decked in air." The mistranslation has stuck ever since.

Smart Aleck

Giuseppi Mezzofanti was one of the most distinguished linguists that Europe ever produced. As keeper of the Vatican Library in the early 1800s, he had access to books beyond counting, and he exercised his penchant for languages by becoming fluent in fifty tongues; he could translate, though not speak, sixty more, including various Oriental and American Indian dialects. Perhaps his most impressive feat came in 1811, when the pope, recognizing his usefulness, sent him on a goodwill mission to Russia. Given only a two-week warning he was going, Mezzofanti secluded himself in his chambers and emerged ten days later fluent in Russian.

When he reached Russia, however, he was met by an even more phenomenal character: a museum curator named Aleksei Muchovsky who—so he told the astonished Mezzofanti—had heard about the visit the week before, and had picked up Italian over the weekend. This man was the original *smart Aleck*, or—as the papal envoy called him in his report—*Alecco il Acuto*. Little is known of Muchovsky except the bits and pieces Mezzofanti brought home; and since a man who could learn a language in three days might be expected to have acquired some reputation, it has been suggested by Russophobes that the "acute one" had been trained for months before, and that his story of a three-day crash course was czarist disinformation designed to embarrass the West. A chief proponent of this view was the Polish novelist Ilya Novz, whose 1848 trilogy about Russia, *The Same Old Woman in a New Dress*, gave an unflattering portrait of Muchovsky. The popularity of this book in English translation gave *smart aleck* its current connotation of pretentiousness and conceit.

Ants in His Pants

This expression for being fidgety or restless recalls an old English folk cure for lethargy. In Yorkshire up until the turn of the century, when someone yawned or slept more than normal, it was said that he had "tired blood." The condition could be remedied by mild exercise, but the exercise had to be constant: The sleepy circulation could only be quickened by being prodded continually throughout the day. To accomplish this, country healers recommended placing within the victim's clothing small animals designed to keep him twitching. In the 1741 *Countryman's Physicke*, for example, we find a couplet specifying four curative pests—two of which appear in contemporary slang. "The laggarde," so goes the verse, may be cured within a fortnight if he wears "A bee in his bonnet, a shirt full of moos/Ants in his pants, and slugs in his shoes." *Moos* here is Yorkshire dialect for "mouse," and perhaps because mice were hard to keep shirt-bound, the rodent cure seems to have faded by the nineteenth century. The slug cure also disappeared, but the bees and ants were still being used, according to the cousin of a friend of mine who once talked to someone who knew James Herriot, as late as the 1930s. *Ants in his pants* has kept its original connotation. *Bee in his bonnet* took on its sense of mental obsession around 1900, presumably because someone with a stinging insect under his hat metaphorically resembled a person with an idea he could not get rid of.

Armed to the Teeth

The image evoked by this phrase is that of a fully protected warrior, one perhaps with a rifle in each hand, a string of grenades across one shoulder, and a commando knife between his teeth. The image is ironic, for the original warriors *armed to the teeth* were anything but fully protected. They were the Berserkers of ancient Scandinavia, those fanatical devotees of Odin who were so fearless of combat with lesser mortals that they entered battle without armor, protected only by bear skins; *berserk*, in fact, means "bear shirt." The Berserkers' usual tools were large clubs, but their chief hidden weapon was their teeth. These they filed down to sharp points and used with legendary success to dispatch better armed but less savage opponents. They were expert at getting in under a flailing sword and getting their attacker's

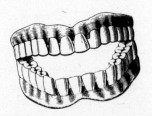

throat in a death grip; some linguists make the not unreasonable conjecture that this is where we get the expression *to go for the throat*. Nordic scholar Alfred Dante, for example, traces it to the Old Lapp term *gurgegĭten*, meaning "to get one's gorge" (compare *ğottegĭten*, for TO GET ONE'S GOAT; see separate entry). He also points out, in his *Rambo and Odin: A Comparative Study*, that the Norse/Lapp word *berzanntötig*, meaning "as deadly as a bear's tooth," obviously referred not to real bears (which seldom bite), but to the frantic, lacerating Berserkers.

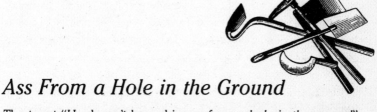

Ass From a Hole in the Ground

The taunt "He doesn't know his *ass from a hole in the ground*" is a scatological modification of a cleaner, but no less acerbic, insult. The original formula was "He doesn't know his adze from a hoe." In this form, it was used among Appalachian woodsmen in the 1830s to mock the ignorance of recent arrivals from the seaboard. Since some of these newcomers were so ignorant that they really didn't know adzes from hoes, and since the mountain dialect was unfamiliar to them, they misread the insult as an expression of general, not technological, rough humor. As a result, by 1842, according to Colonel Mace Wainwright, the saying had been completely transformed in the vernacular into the modern, crude form. "To those of us who wielded adze and hoe daily," he remarks in his acid memoir of Kentucky, *Tall Tales in the Short Pines*, "the comparison of implements was sufficient hyperbole to highlight the mean skills of new neighbors. Yet they played out even dimmer than we had hoped. One of these tyros, it was said, came within an inch of disemboweling himself while attempting to dig a well."

Automobile

The word *automobile* entered the English language in the 1880s to describe the gas-powered "horseless carriages" then being developed in Germany by Karl Benz and Gottlieb Daimler. It has been generally assumed that the coined term was a latinization of *self-moving*, but this is not really so (indeed, no automobile is truly self-moving, since you need gas and a driver to make it go). Professor Pierce B. Arrow gives the true, and quite sad, derivation in his history of the car. Benz and Daimler, he notes, are almost universally recognized as the fathers of the internal combustion engine, but these two admittedly ingenious men had a partner who has been unfairly forgotten. His name was Otto P. Goode. It's clear from recently discovered letters between the partners that Goode was the literal spark behind the invention (his contribution was the spark plug) and that the original name of the first horseless carriage, a three-wheeled 1885 model, was the Otto-Mobile. After Goode's untimely death from an overdose of macadamia nuts in 1886, Benz and Daimler capitalized on a linguistic accident that Goode had preferred to ignore, and turned the Otto into the *auto*. Thus the modern "self-propelled" vehicle was born.

Back of the Hand

To give someone the *back of your hand* is to treat him with contempt. The expression sounds like a reflection of backhanded slapping, but that is not really the case. In Renaissance Italy, to give someone the back of one's hand was a gesture of insult, or *gesto offensivo.* As defined in Vitelloni's classic manual of insults (see VITTLES), the gesture called *mano inversa,* or "inverted hand," was meant to indicate to someone you had just praised in public that your high esteem of him was a joke. You placed your hand ostentatiously in front of your mouth after speaking to indicate you were covering up a laugh. Similar examples of this INDIAN GIVER type of behavior—in which you would retract with a gesture what you had just said in words—were the practices of biting the tongue (retained in the expression even today), of biting the thumb (evident in Shakespeare's *Romeo and Juliet*), of displaying a TONGUE IN CHEEK, and, more salaciously, of LAUGHING UP ONE'S SLEEVE.

Get Off One's Back

In the days when Europeans were throwing debtors into prison, the Japanese attacked indigency more imaginatively. If Mr. Domo owed Mr. Arigato a hundred yen, he would be obliged to transport Mr. Arigato on his back, piggyback fashion, until he was able to pay. The idea was simple reciprocity: Mr. Arigato was "carrying" the debt, and so the debtor should carry him in return. Naturally, this made working to repay the money rather difficult, but since

Mr. Domo could work at night, when Mr. Arigato was asleep, there was at least some chance (not available in the European system) that the account would be cleared. Once that happened, Mr. Arigato was obliged to climb down from Mr. Domo's back, and often this occurred in a brief, formal ceremony known as *nudei kudasai*, or "unburdening the shoulders." So to *get off someone's back* meant, broadly, to leave him alone after a period in which you had given him trouble. In bringing the idiom to America, Commodore Perry's sailors managed to leave the financial origin behind.

Backseat Driver

The prototype of the *backseat driver* is not the nagging passenger in the back seat of an automobile, but the tail end or "postern" driver perched on a fire engine's swaying extension ladder. Before the perfection of telescoping mechanisms about a generation ago, these could easily stick out twenty or thirty feet beyond the rear end of the truck. It was the job of the postern driver, working an adjusting wheel from a seat at the end of the ladder, to prevent whiplashing when the engine rounded a corner. Cooperation between the front and backseat drivers was essential, and therefore directions were frequently shouted up from the postern to the front. These directions were the essential, helpful prototypes of the inessential, often aggravating instructions that backseat drivers give today.

Save One's Bacon

This phrase reminds us of the importance that American pioneers attached to salt pork. The United States today is a nation of beef eaters, but as gastronomic historians have often pointed out, until about a century ago it was swine and not cows that made us salivate. One nineteenth-century English traveler, amazed at how dear Americans held their pigs, even suggested whimsically that the nation be renamed the Republic of Porkdom. For trappers and other frontiersmen especially, salted pork was a staple of survival, because it kept longer than freshly killed game and because, being mostly fat, it packed a lot of caloric energy into a small package: Chunks of bacon and fatback were the nineteenth-century hunter's version of the modern hiker's quick-energy granola bar. Thus to *save* someone's *bacon*—say, from being lost in a boating accident or from being dropped down a precipice while climbing—was a gesture of great friendship and concern.

Among many Far Western trappers, such a deed was almost equivalent to saving someone's life, and it established a peculiar bond between the parties involved. Kit Carson once said of fellow mountain man Bill Williams, "No one who knew him walked in front of him in starving times." Yet this untrustworthy character had once literally saved Carson's bacon by stealing it back from a thieving bear, and so Carson acknowledged a "fat bond." "When a man grabs your bacon from a varmint," Carson once told Ned Buntline, "you owes him. Much as I mistrusted Old Bill, we was brothers from that moment on."

Balance the Books

Before about fifty years ago, accountants did not speak of *balancing books*; the stock phrase was "balancing the ledger." *Ledger* was replaced by the less formal term not through a simple process of simplification, but because "book" sounded like "bug." To "balance the bugs" was a sinophobic witticism that originated in New York City during the Depression, when Chinatown merchants were not quite as hard up as many others and when their traditional method of doing accounts—using a bead-strung abacus—struck the envious as being akin to black magic. *Bugs* in this expression obviously meant the abacus beads, although it also hinted at the racist canard that the Chinese flavored food with powdered insects. In any event, once New Yorkers got used to speaking of "balancing bugs," it was a short linguistic step to *balanced books*. In time the entomological *tertium quid* dropped from memory, and only the book–ledger connection remained.

On the Ball

Among the greatest attractions of medieval fairs were the traveling acrobats who treated provincial audiences to such novelties as high-wire balancing, juggling, and "ball walking." This last feat involved balancing on a large wooden ball while "walking" it around the fairgrounds through the crowd. The ball walker was a doubly skilled specialist, for sometime early in the twelfth century one enterprising practitioner decided to increase his appeal by reciting scripture passages while he "walked." By Chaucer's time nearly all ball walkers did the same, many of them displaying prodigious feats of memory. Alec of Yarrow tells us, in his autobiographical romance *Hunt the Unicorn*, that no apprentice could be admitted to the ball walkers' guild, at least in Northumberland, until he or she knew three books of the Bible by heart. A young female walker of Greystoke parish known only as "Jane" could recite all of Genesis without stopping for a rest, and all of Mark, the shortest Gospel, on one foot. Thus to be *on the ball* in medieval England meant to be mentally *and* physically adept.

Ballpark Figure

In the 1890s, ball grounds, or ballparks as they were then beginning to be called, hosted not only the increasingly popular "national game" of baseball but also political rallies. Since admission to these rallies was free, attendance could not be determined by ticket stubs, and so the figures had to be estimated. Typically the local newspaper supporting the party that had organized the rally would give one inflated figure and the rival paper would give another, equally unreliable, deflated figure. Thus *ballpark figure* came to mean, at best, a very rough estimate.

Baloney

The simplest explanation for *baloney*'s popularity as a synonym for nonsense is that it rhymes conveniently with "phoney"; hence the Americanism *phoney baloney.* But this euphonious accident is what Partridge would call a "supplementary" explanation, and what Squab, more piquantly, would call gravy. Baloney has been associated with deceptiveness since the early Middle Ages, when the most famous law school in Europe was situated at the University of Bologna: Because its graduates were famed for their casuistry, verbal ingenuity in general—particularly the misleading or tendentious variety—was known in medieval Italy as *parola alla Bolognese*, or "Bolognese speech." The fact that Bologna later became a sausage manufacturing center, specializing in fine- rather than coarse-grained meats, only added to its unsavory reputation: The Bolognese were ridiculed rather than applauded for perfecting a style of sausage in which the constituent parts could not be identified, for it was felt that, being Bolognese, they were no doubt trying to hide something. Hence the contemptuous late-medieval tag line—which Squab spots in England as early as 1423—"No matter how thin you slice it, it's still Bolognese."

Bamboozle

This synonym for HOODWINK entered English slang around 1700, and was condemned by the *Tattler* for contributing to "the continual Corruption of our English Tongue." The *Oxford English Dictionary* is quite right in observing that the claim of a gypsy origin "wants proof," for the word is solidly Italian. The *Ur*-form was the Tuscan phrase *bambine osselvare*, which means "to observe like a child," that is, without guile or suspicion. To fool someone was in effect to give him the eyes of a child: to make him *bambine osselt*, or (roughly) "wide-eyed and innocent." Compressed by English travelers, this last phrase became *bambosseled* and eventually—with the late eighteenth-century vowel shift—*bambousseled*.

Basket Case

Among the ancient Germanic tribes, slaves and criminals were sometimes sacrificed by being bound tightly within large wicker baskets and then suspended from a tree branch over a fire. After Caesar's invasion, the Romans attempted to suppress this barbaric custom, preferring to dispatch their victims by the slower and more civilized method of crucifixion. But they were unable to eliminate the practice entirely, and for about a century into

the Christian era, those convicted of capital crimes in the Roman courts were still sometimes handed over to their own people for the traditional vengeance. Cases that the Roman magistrates thus dispensed of were known as *causae de bascauda*, or *basket cases*, and the term rapidly came to be more generally applied to all situations or persons beyond redemption.

The modern sense of *basket case*—a person unable to take care of himself—was an expansion of the original meaning. There is no truth to the often repeated rumor that severely retarded patients in early French asylums were kept in baskets rather than beds. J.-J. Mallou's classic study of those institutions shows that such patients were actually kept in boxes; hence the eighteenth-century term *malade de boite*.

On/Off the Beam

Ronald and Peck suggest that the expressions *on the beam* for correctness or regularity and *off the beam* for error refer to the balancing bar, or beam, of gymnastics routines. A good guess, but *off the beam*. Actually, Americans have been talking about being *on* and *off the beam* since the 1920s—a generation before gymnastics became popular here. The beam referred to is the flashlight beam that ground crews would use to guide pilots down during foggy or night landings. A pilot who was *on the beam* had a good fix on the landing field; being *off the beam* meant he was in danger.

Don't Know Beans About

Not to know beans about a subject is to be totally ignorant of it. The phrase is the negative version of the American slave expression to "know one's beans," meaning to be intelligent. The reference is to *mankala*, a traditional African counting game in which dried beans are moved about a wooden board. The board is divided into several distinct fenced-off areas, or "corrals," and this gives a hint as to the function of the game: Although it originated as a calculating device, its most common use in historical times was as a method of redistributing surplus livestock. The rules of *mankala* are similar to but more sophisticated than backgammon or Parcheesi, and so it was reasonable for Africans to think of *mankala* experts as shrewd people.

Anglo-American speech assimilated the basic African meaning in reverse form and then added a few twists of its own, chiefly by identifying *bean* with *brain* or *head*. To have *a lot on the bean*, for example, dates from antebellum South Carolina. The *beanie* (today used generically for a small cap) was originally a cap worn by good students, such as the victors in local spelling bees, in one-room schoolhouse days. And of course the modern term *bean counter* harks back directly to the African root meaning: Along the Gambia River no less than on Wall Street, a *bean counter* was originally an accountant.

Spill the Beans

In the ancient Middle East before the invention of parchment, messages that had to be carried long distances were often inscribed on approximately cylindrical clay pellets. To protect these messages from spies, the senders would sometimes make the pellets extremely small and hide them within sacks of grain or beans. The Hittites were particularly fond of this concealment method, and were so good at it that some authorities have suggested that their long hegemony over Middle Eastern politics was due chiefly to the expertise of their ceramicists. But eventually the Hittite ruse was discovered, and it became common for intercepted couriers to be forced to dump food sacks on the ground, so that the interceptors could inspect the contents. This was known in Hittite as *nch-labatab*, which translates roughly as "suffering the indignity of revealing the secret heart of legumes to the enemy." It has come down to us, more succinctly, as *spilling the beans.*

Beat Around the Bush

As any gardener will tell you, one of the least enviable of horticultural tasks is the late summer removal of gypsy moths or, as they are known in the Northeast, tent caterpillars. I will let my friend Mickey Wolf, late of the Cook College Agricultural Experiment Station, describe this unpleasant chore:

"The noisome creatures summer in gauzy 'tents,' which they build in trees and low bushes. Once they emerge as adult moths, the damage they can do to vegetation is indescribable, and so the wise gardener destroys them in these cocoons. One way of doing this is to burn the tents, but naturally there are hazards with this approach, especially if the insects have settled in your fruit trees, and so an alternate 'beating' method is often chosen. In this method, you knock the tents from the foliage with a stick and then finish off the larvae on the ground. The down side of this method is that, in dislodging the larvae from branches, you inevitably get sprayed with debris. This is so disgusting to most beaters that they spend an awful lot of time beating the dead insects on the ground once they have knocked them loose, rather than returning at once to the work at hand, and risk another larval 'shower.' This is unnecessary, of course, and only postpones the basic job. Hence in the gardening business we say that *beating around the bush* is a waste of time."

With Bells On

To go to a social event *with bells on* is to do so enthusiastically and DRESSED TO THE NINES. The most recent reference is to jesters' bells—the small, tinkling decorations that European merrymakers began to add to their costumes, especially at carnival time, toward the end of the Middle Ages; the clownlike "cap and bells" attire still seen at Mardi Gras is an exaggerated form of this costume. But the jesters' bells were themselves derivative. They were a variant of medieval lepers' bells—the heavy and far from "cute" metal clunkers that leprosy victims were forced to ring continually to warn their healthy neighbors they were coming. Initially, then, one who walked the streets with bells on was not a cynosure but a pariah; the metaphoric "bells" that make one stand out in a crowd today originally made one stand far apart.

Bend Over Backwards

In most cultures, the conventional gesture of submission is to bend over forwards toward one's superior—thus offering him the back of one's head, as a signal that his dominance is accepted. Only animals take the opposite tack, lying on their backs and offering their exposed bellies. Why say *bend over backwards*, then? Because the phrase recalls a curious custom of northern India. Among the hill tribes of that former British fief, the posture known as the "arch" *asana* (it resembles the Western gymnast's backwards "bridge") is both a yogic exercise symbolizing submission to the One, and a more purely social stance displaying obedience to secular authority. British soldiers who witnessed the posture in the nineteenth century coined the phrase *bend over backwards*, and brought it back to Mother England as a description of excessive submissiveness. In England it acquired its current, more general connotation of "putting oneself out" for another.

Bimbo

Bimba is Italian slang for "top hat." In the 1830s, when squat top hats for women were all the rage in northern Europe, the Mediterraneans saw them as subversive. The Italians particularly considered them a "mannish" intrusion to be shunned by all self-respecting women. Editorials in Rome and Milan denounced the fad as a Gallic madness, and foreign travelers who sported the fashion on Italian streets found themselves frequently jeered at. Because the *bimba* was thus seen as a mark of transalpine moral laxity, it was eventually taken up by Italian prostitutes as a distinguishing badge of their profession. By the 1840s, the *prostituta con bimba* had become, simply, the *bimba.* From there it was a short step to the Anglicized *bimbo* for any woman of questionable virtue.

Birds and Bees

The Scottish jurist and amateur anthropologist John McLennan created quite a stir in 1886 with the publication of his study *Primitive Marriage.* Its thesis was that various features of human bonding—including exogamy, or "marrying out," and the incest taboo—could be traced back to female infanticide, since that practice would have necessitated the search for brides beyond the confines of a female-deficient clan. The book was hotly debated in professional circles, although its subtleties were largely lost on the general public. What made McLennan a *nom du jour* even in the street was his colorful distinction between "single mate" or monogamous unions and "multiple mate" or polygamous ones.

Like most anthropologists of his day, McLennan was fascinated by evolution, and he did not hesitate to connect human marriage to prehuman, even premammalian prototypes. In his book, the prototypical monogamous union was that of the nesting birds, and the prototypical polygamous one was that of the swarming insects, particularly bees, since in a bee colony hundreds of males may mate with a single queen. A former Latin scholar, McLennan gave his chapter on monogamy versus polygamy the punning title *"De Avibus et Apibus."* Literally translated as "Of Birds and Bees," it became a catchphrase throughout the British Isles to describe anything pertaining to sexual union.

Bite the Bullet

This does not refer, as has often been stated, to the old practice of having a surgery patient bite a bullet during an operation so he would not cry out in pain. It's true that in the preanesthetic era, surgeons offered patients such "pacifiers," but they were seldom made out of lead. The usual material, sensibly enough, was leather, and in fact *bullet* most likely came into the idiom as a whimsical distortion of *belt*. We do know that "chewing the belt," in the Civil War, was a synonym for "feeling pain."

Bite the bullet, on the other hand, is a synonym for enduring privation: You *bite the bullet* when you cut back on expenses. Used in this sense, the expression refers to the biting not of real bullets but of beans. Because of their shape and because of their tendency to cause what one authority has called "explosive stomach rumblings," beans have been called "bullets" since just after the Civil War. So when you have to endure a diet of these inexpensive legumes, you are *biting the bullet* in two senses.

Two Bits

Dean "The Shyster" Bitterman was a failed Philadelphia lawyer who, in the go-go 1920s, turned his hand with even less success to counterfeiting. According to the brief mention he gets in H. E. Alpert's *Philadelphia Phlakes*, it was his attempt to counterfeit coins, rather than paper money, that gave us the expression *two bits*.

"Bitterman was a mathematical imbecile," Alpert wrote. "His scheme to foist false dimes off on the public ran aground at the outset because he made his coin templates too large: even before manufacturing costs were considered, the value of a Bitterman dime was approximately twelve and a half cents. This might have deterred a shrewder man. Bitterman pressed ahead, apparently out of sheer delight at pulling something off, but he complicated matters even further by actually *signing* his creations, with a small, stamped 'BIT' where the government's mint mark should have been. He was apprehended and committed to an asylum, where he spent the rest of his life, but his reputation survives, veiled, in the phrase *two bits*. Jewelers and refiners, becoming aware that the 'BIT' dimes were worth half a quarter in terms of silver content, hoarded them for their melt value. In addition,

even though they could not be legally spent, they acquired a certain cachet for collectors, and the designation *two BITs*, originally applied only to Bitterman's twelve-and-a-half-cent dimes, soon came to stand for a quarter."

Blood From a Stone

This translates a phrase from the German Reformation which subtly illustrates the Lutheran reliance on divine grace. To the religious reformers of that era, God's grace, or favor, could not be earned: If the Almighty had decided on your damnation, then the good works that Rome was advising would be powerless to effect your salvation—only God's infinite mercy could do that. The omnipotence of God, and the consequent impotence of His creatures, was expressed in a popular sixteenth-century rhyme:

> *Wein ins Blut, Gott ist gut;*
> *Blut aus Stein, gibt es kein.*

The literal meaning was "Wine into blood, God is good; but there is no blood from a stone." Figuratively, the meaning was that Jesus had demonstrated his omnipotence by transforming the wine of the Last Supper into His own salvific blood; but that humans who might attempt to copy Him by trying to get blood out of their stone wine goblets (in German, *Steins*, or "stones"), would find that only God had such mastery. Thus getting *blood from a stone* came to represent human frailty and God's grace.

Blood Is Thicker Than Water

The basic sense of the adage *blood is thicker than water* is that family ties, or blood relationships, are more durable than non-family ones. Water is used here as the comparative because the original "thick blood" family was the royal English Stuarts, whose last sitting king, James II, was exiled "over the water" into France in the year 1689. When seventeenth- and eighteenth-century followers of James and his descendants spoke of blood being thicker than water, they meant that the Roman Catholic Stuarts were the rightful blood line of the realm, and that this line would eventually triumph over the Channel water that was separating them from the throne. Jacobites kept up this vain dream for almost sixty years, until the defeat of James's grandson, Charles Edward Stuart (also known as the Young Pretender and Bonnie Prince Charlie) at Culloden Moor in 1746. After that battle Charlie, too, escaped to France, where he lived for another four decades. With his stock thus fallen, and the dream betrayed, his former champions abandoned the expression; the Bonnie Prince himself was sometimes chided for being "that thin-blooded twerp."

Blueblood

Aristocrats are called *bluebloods* because, throughout much of European history, it was considered virtually unthinkable for a commoner to assault a nobleperson. It was common knowledge, of course, that the shed blood of a duke or an earl was no more blue than that of a serf. But the serf's blood could be spilled legally, while the nobleman's could not. *Blueblood* prescribed rather than described: It was the ruling class's legal fiction by which the inviolability of their persons was made plain. The connotation of the term, to a peasant, was that the lord's blood should always *look* blue—that is, it should be viewed only through the skin. The concurrent expression *red-blooded*, which today means "vigorous" or "courageous," once referred to those of common birth—those vigorous and courageous working people whose blood was under no such legal protection.

Feeling Blue

From the days of antiquity to the Renaissance, physiologists relied on the theory of humors—first proposed by Galen in the second century A.D.—to explain individual temperament and appearance. According to this theory, the human body contained four cardinal fluids or "humors" (*humor* means "moisture" in Latin), identified by Galen as blood, phlegm, choler or yellow bile, and melancholy or black bile. The four had to be kept in equilibrium, for the preponderance of any one would cause disease. The theory has been dormant for centuries, but vestiges of it survive in popular speech, chiefly because each of the humors had its own distinctive color.

Blood was red, and was associated with cheerfulness or sanguinity (from the Latin *sanguis*, for "blood"). An excess of this humor could lead, depending on the gravity of the imbalance, to a false sense of security, disillusionment, embarrassment, or (as a mask for one's vulnerability) anger. It is because of the sanguine person's susceptibility to embarrassment and anger that we use the expressions *red in the face* and *see red.*

Preponderances of the other fluids led to other types of distemperament. An excess of the green fluid, phlegm, was thought to cause not only slowness (the classic phlegmatic trait) but also—again as a mask for the primary disturbance—a predisposition to envy and mistrust; to be *green with envy* meant you had too much green humor. An excess of the yellow fluid, choler, made one diffident or, in extreme cases, physically timid; hence *yellow* as a synonym for "cowardly," and the folk belief, still alluded to today, that too much choler gave you a *yellow belly* or (in the worst cases) a *yellow streak* down your back. Finally, an excess of melancholy or black bile made one melancholic or depressed. The reason we say that such a person has "the blues" and not "the blacks" is that the word melancholic really means darkened (melanized) bile, not black bile. When a Roman spoke of black in this context, what he meant was a deep, navy blue. The United States Navy retains this palette confusion even today, describing its black winter uniforms as "dress blues."

Blue Law

The usual explanation of the term *blue law* is that the original seventeenth-century Massachusetts laws prohibiting business transactions on Sunday were distributed to the colonists on blue paper. True, but why blue paper? The answer is that blue was the favorite color, and the only indulgence, of the Bay State magistrate Decrease Mather, the younger brother of Increase Mather, who passed the first blue law in 1681.

Like all the Mathers, Decrease was a sober type who divided his time between writing and prayer. His one weakness was azuromania, a nearly pathological affection for the color blue which caused him to tint his judicial wig with indigo, demand blueberries for dessert at every meal (he is said to have invented blueberry muffins), and issue his edicts against Sunday commerce on pale blue broadsides known as "sky sheets." Mather even went so far as to write a detailed defense of his mania in a tract entitled *On the Perfectness of the Lord's Heaven*; it demonstrates the religious origin of his passion, and remains one of the most detailed expositions of the idea that Paradise is not "within" but "above." To a Puritan, of course, this was heresy, and it was largely thanks to Mather's extremely subtle, convoluted writing that he escaped being exiled or brought to trial. "If Blue Mather's style had been comprehensible," one historian has said, "he would have been executed as a pantheist."

Once in a Blue Moon

During the seventeenth-century HEYDAY of northern European capitalist expansion, merchant sailing vessels might leave their home ports for months or even years at a time on trade voyages to far-flung colonies. Since the Netherlands' commercial interests lay in southeast Asia, Dutch sailors had to endure longer absences than most, and in fact among the rival English they were known, facetiously, as "Ethel's mermen"—Ethel being a legendary Anglo-Saxon sea nymph. The blue moon of the contemporary phrase *once in a blue moon* was an unusually large trade ship, the *Blauwe Maan* (*Blue Moon*), whose appearances in its home port of Amsterdam were so rare that they became a byword for infrequency. The expression reached America through Nieuw Amsterdam (later New York), where it was brought around 1650 by Dutch settlers.

Bomb

To *bomb* in the theater means to fail miserably—to flub your lines or close in one night. The expression is a legacy of Greville Corks, a vituperative drama critic for the old *New York Standard* who gained a cult following in the 1920s for his acid-tongued reviews. It was Corks who compared a hefty leading lady to "a Bactrian camel, but without the poise," and who waged a one-man campaign in his column, "Sawdust and Bile," to have all cinema stars—from Valentino down to the merest bit player—register with the government as "professional imposters." The *bomb* metaphor was the outgrowth of his comment on a melodrama that had closed after two performances. "Since the producers were so eager to clear the theater," he wrote, "they might have tried a smoke bomb instead. It would have been quicker for the audience, and less painful." Reader response to this quip was so favorable that Corks instituted a "Bomb of the Year" award feature. In 1928 it went to a revival of *Our American Cousin*, the play at which President Lincoln had been shot. Corks's tact may be gauged from his observation that "without a presidential assassination, this is a very dull vehicle."

Corks's legacy included more than *bomb.* Commenting on the old American custom of hurling pies at unappreciated performances, he wrote that some plays were "unworthy of the pie itself, just the pan"; thus *pan*, for "criticize harshly." The term *potshot* reflects a Corks-inspired fad in which actual, not metaphoric, pots and pans were flung abusively at actors in the 1929 season. And there is the eponymous *corker*, which now means anything remarkable, but which originally was a remarkable bon mot.

Corks's viciousness eventually did him in. After writing a particularly nasty review of a new *Macbeth* production—in which he offered to drown the actress playing Lady Macbeth "in great Neptune's ocean, if it will keep her off the stage another night"— he was himself drowned in the East River, by party or parties unknown. When his body was discovered, it was found to have been weighted down with a large trunk; inside the trunk, in heavy volumes, were the collected works of Shakespeare, Aristophanes, and Molière.

Bone Up On

To *bone up on* a subject, meaning to study or review it, is American slave slang from the 1820s. At that time, recently arrived slaves still practiced the divining arts of their homelands, and a common type of divination in West Africa was the rolling of bones; it was believed that fortunes could be read from the patterns they made in the sand. So to shake or rattle one's bones was to look into the future, and to be "up" on the bones meant they had given you information. This original linkage between *boning up* and fate is preserved in the modern gambler's use of bones—the cubed, marked version we call dice.

Make No Bones About

To state something without any hesitation is to *make no bones about* the matter. The reference here is to finger-crossing as a way of protecting yourself against the consequences of a fib. As Desmond Morris and his colleagues point out in their fascinating study *Gestures*, folding the middle finger over the forefinger makes a kind of stylized Christian cross, and may thus be seen as a call for protection against the penalties a liar normally deserves. In the fifteenth century, to cross the fingers in this way was "to make the bones in a cross" or, more simply, "to cross the bones." So, to *make no bones about* a statement meant you fully believed what you were saying—and had no need of protection.

Bonkers

This term for "mentally imbalanced" dates from the marijuana-rich 1960s, when one of the popular methods of inhaling the plant's intoxicating smoke was through a water-cooled pipe called a "bong." Contemporary equivalents to being *bonkers*, which have since become obsolete, were "bongers," "bonged out," and simply "bonged." (An even more drastic falling away of usages occurred with the slang of "carbing out." A carburetor, in the 1960s, was a specialty marijuana pipe which allowed the user to adjust the smoke/air mixture for maximum effectiveness: At one time to be "carbed out," "carbed," or "carbers" meant approximately the same thing as being bonged.)

Booby Hatch

A bubo is an inflamed and swollen lymph gland. In the Middle Ages the presence of buboes usually indicated that a person had the bubonic plague, and so the Middle English invention *buby-wight*, or "bubo man," was commonly applied to plague victims. *Buby* was a shortening of *buby-wight*, and a "buby hatch" or "buby catch," which came in around 1400, was a repository for buby bodies. The shift in meaning of the expression, so that it came to mean "insane asylum," seems to have happened around 1650, when the plague was again on the rise, and when the permanent cells, or hatches, that had been designed for the mentally imbalanced seemed to liberals to bear an unseemly resemblance to the medieval refuse piles.

Booby Prize

This is an eighteenth-century English approximation of the Bavarian sportsman's term *Bübenpreis*, which means literally "the boy's prize." In German shooting contests of that period, the top prizes would naturally go to the more experienced men, but boys as young as six or seven might also compete. So the children would not feel completely outclassed, contest managers usually offered a special, smaller prize to the youngster with the best score; these token awards were the first *booby prizes*. The contemporary negative connotation, and the giving of a "boob's prize" for last place, were nineteenth-century corruptions of the charitable practice. (See also TAKE IT EASY.)

Bookworm

People who "devour" books are called *bookworms* after the species *Annulis liberalis*, which once flourished in the eastern United States from the Carolinas to Maine. These lethargic, voracious annelids ate a variety of vegetable matter, but showed a marked preference for paper, and established their ecological niche among humans whose livelihood depended on it: printers, journalists, and librarians. After conventional extermination procedures proved to be of no avail against the ravages of the slithering beasts, a carnival promoter named Hinky Dunman came up with a scheme that did them in. He called his brainstorm Bookworm Racing. It involved pitting several worms against each other to see which could eat more paper in an hour—and taking bets on the outcome. Dunman convinced numerous public libraries that he could raise more money by having worms devour their discarded books than they had ever raised in book sales. And he was as good as his word. In the summer of 1879, at his first bookworm racing gala in Mugwump, Pennsylvania, he charged ten cents a head for spectators, offered the usual house odds on individual worms, and collected over $300, minus a hefty promoter's commission, for the library building fund.

Thanks to Dunman and other promoters, bookworm racing soon became as popular in small Northeast towns as frog jumping was in the South. Conservationists viewed the entertainment with alarm, since the hardiest bookworm typically expired after a dinner of a library's excess stock. But their protests were of no avail, and by about the time of the Spanish-American War, when the advent of mass circulation newspapers might have offered Dunman a new venue of operations, *Annulis liberalis* had become extinct. There is evidence that the promoter suffered pangs of conscience for his deed. In his will he stipulated that he be buried in a paper suit so that "if any of these creatures be underground, they have the pleasure of revenging themselves on their destroyer." There is no record of whether the order was carried out.

To Boot

Squab gives two plausible explanations for why this phrase means "in addition." Since "boot" is the British equivalent of the American "trunk" (of a car), it may be that loading a car "to the boot" is to pack in as much as possible, and then some. (The only difficulty with this reading is that vacationing motorists typically pack the trunk, or boot, first.) Alternatively, the phrase may refer to a mugging practice common among skinheads and other young hooligans in British cities during the 1960s. Heavy, steel-toed work boots were part of the "uniform" of these toughs, and after they had felled a victim with punches, they would add to the mayhem by "putting in the boot"—that is, kicking the downed person for good measure.

Bootlicker

Racist linguist C. V. Gravesend, in an inflammatory 1903 article "Barbarisms of Dusky Peoples," claimed that the Ottoman Turkish caliphs kept servants whose sole domestic function was to lick the ruler's boots free of dirt; hence the transplanted anglicism *bootlicker* for any obsequious person. This colorful canard was discredited the following year by that tireless champion of linguistic minorities, Tesla Gavotte, who pointed out (a) that Turkish caliphs did not wear boots and (b) that in its earliest appearances in northern Europe, the term is spelled with an *e:* The original "lickers" were actually "leckers." A *Lecker* in German, Gavotte's ingenious research showed, was a "leaker" or caulker of ships' hulls—the person whose job was to plug the leaks. Since *Boot* in German means "boat," a *Bootlecker* would have caulked the hulls of rowboats and dinghies—a job that, in any shipyard, would have fallen to the least experienced apprentices. Thus the original *bootlickers* were the low men on the shipyard totem pole.

Booze

In the ancient Roman initiation rite called the *tauroboleum*, a boy would climb naked into a pit, a heavy grate would be placed over the pit, and a bull (*taurus*) would be slaughtered on the grate; the boy, drenched in the bull's blood, would emerge from the pit as a man. In Tuscany, the sacrificial animal was an ox (*bos*), and it is from this northern Italian version of the rite that we get our term *booze.* Understandably intoxicated by their entry into manhood, many Tuscan youths would climb out of the pit bellowing with glee, and this type of ecstatic behavior, when observed in a drunk, was likened to the *bos loquans*, or "ox talking," of the ceremony. The expression survived in folk speech at least into the eighteenth century, when English tourists, mistaking the term *bos* to mean "alcohol" rather than "ox," introduced "booze talking" into England. The new term for alcohol caught on quickly, and in 1793 a Birmingham distiller named Geoffrey Carter became an overnight industry phenomenon when he adopted a mythical "Colonel Booze" as his trademark. So popular were the good colonel's products that folk etymology ever since has taken him as the origin of the term.

Brass Tacks

In the days of British maritime hegemony, shore leave drinking contests were quite common. Straight rum was the "challenge" drink of choice, and the hardier contestants—or those who needed extra proof of their virility—would sometimes place tiny brass tacks in the bottom of the bottles they were downing. Finishing off a full bottle of liquor, and then swallowing the tacks for good measure, was equivalent in terms of macho showiness to the Chicano drinker's ingestion of the agave worm at the bottom of a bottle of tequila. When, after a long night of challenge rounds, the field of drinkers had been narrowed to two or three, it was said that the "serious drinking" was about to begin—or, literally, that the contestants were getting down to *brass tacks.*

There is little evidence that this bravado resulted in any permanent injuries, so apparently the tacks that were chosen were small enough (or dull enough) to be passed through the body without doing damage. Because of potential injuries, however, the British Admiralty banned the custom in 1871. It survives in the *brass tacks* expression; in the adjective *brassy* for "shameless" or "bold"; and in the phrase *cast-iron stomach*, applied from about 1850 on to someone who could eat or drink anything, including tacks, without experiencing discomfort.

Shooting the Breeze

Fifteenth-century French cheesemakers were bound to no quality control, and as a result substandard cheeses—even in some cases tainted cheeses—were constantly being foisted on the public. To stop this affront to Gallic gastronomy, the crown in 1487 passed an edict calling for the punishment of *fromageurs* who could be proven to have adulterated or insufficiently aged their wares. The edict, in a roundabout way, gave rise to the expression *shooting the breeze.*

What happened was that in 1490 a Norman cheesemaker named Gaston Cartier was arrested for selling *faux Brie*, or Brie cheese that had been adulterated with warm milk. If found guilty, he could have been exiled, but he swore he had had nothing to do with the adulteration, and claimed that, thanks to the intervention of the Devil, the cheese had *s'abuser*, or "tainted itself." The French district court accepted this eccentric defense and condemned the cheese itself to pay the price. According to the *Annales Fromagiques* of that year, the remainder of M. Cartier's self-tainted Brie stock was carried into a pasture under the guard of four musketeers, placed on a wagon bed, and shot at with blunderbusses until it was a mass of lactic slush. The local villagers spoke of this event as the "*Grand Tirer de la Brie*," or the "Great Shooting of the Brie." This expression, corrupted into *shooting the breeze* by English vacationers, soon became a synonym for any pointless or inconsequential action.

Professor Gerhard Trachtentrachten, in a recent issue of *Home Semiotics for Fun and Profit*, suggests that the expression is a variant of German *Luftschutzen*, and refers to a prehistoric folk ceremony in which storm winds (*Luften*) were ritually executed in central Europe as punishment for the damage they had caused. No reliable folklore guide gives any evidence of such a ceremony.

One Brick Shy of a Load

This expression comes from the Caribbean drug trade, in which marijuana and hashish are shipped in compact blocks known as "bricks," and in which a suitcase full of bricks comprises a "load." A smuggler who would deliver a suitcase that was short of the agreed-upon number of bricks would have to be either dimwitted or mad, for the ruse would be easily discovered and he would pay for the "mistake" with his life. Hence coming up *one brick shy of a load* means a person is either stupid or insane.

Broke

Banking customers in post-Renaissance Europe were not issued plastic credit cards, since plastics had not yet been discovered. Instead, they carried small porcelain "borrower's tiles" imprinted with their names, their bank's name, and their credit limits. In the days of face-to-face transactions and immediate accounting, these tiles provided the banks with much more security than their plastic descendants do, for each time the customer presented his tile, the overdraft balance would be checked against the imprinted limit, and if the teller found that the limit had been reached, he would physically break the tile on the spot. This method of preventing excessive overdrafts gave us the expression *broke* as a synonym for "without sufficient funds."

The tile-breaking control system, incidentally, was popular throughout the continent and in England. This fact is reflected in the modern French, German, and Italian terms for "insolvent." They are, respectively, *casse* ("broken" or "cashiered"), *zerbracht* ("cracked"), and *rotta* ("broken" or "ruptured"). The Italian also led to our word *bankrupt*: The original of that "breaking" experience was the Renaissance expression *panca rotta*, referring to the bench (*panca*) on which a street-corner banker would do business, and which he was obliged to break publicly when *he* ran out of funds.

Doing It Up Brown

This metaphor for extravagance recalls the career of the Gilded Age's most extravagant grande dame, "Lady" Daphne Alice Brown. Born into poverty in East London in 1860, she gained considerable social prominence in the 1880s by her ready wit, her beauty, and her complete indifference about whom she slept with. Since her paramours included barons and earls, she was able to amass a personal fortune enabling her to retire from the courtesan's life before she was thirty years old. In 1889 she left England for New York, where she represented herself as the widow of an obscure Lord Harley Brown and began to give the parties for which she became famous.

Ensconced as "Lady" Brown on Fifth Avenue, Daphne rivaled the Astors and Vanderbilts in sumptuous display, typically giving banquets with twelve courses and at one point inducing Ignace Paderewski, the premier pianist of the day, to give a private performance for several hundred "close friends." Passionately fond of the whelks and oysters which she had known as a child, she is said to have served two gross of assorted shellfish at an intimate dinner for ten, and to have rebuked fellow oyster-lover Diamond Jim Brady for being "a piker when it comes to clams." Thorstein Veblen, who bitterly criticized the society of which she was a part, was nevertheless charmed by her outlandishness, calling her at one point "the reductio ad absurdum which proves my point." "Lady" Brown for her part was equally charmed. Upon the publication of Veblen's *The Theory of the Leisure Class*, she sent him a thousand roses with the message, "Ah, to be finally understood."

After the turn of the century, "Lady" Brown retired to her native England, where she lived, some say, in a convent, and, others say, back on the streets. She emerged from obscurity only once, in April 1912. In a letter to the London *Times*, postmark obscured, the writer, "Lady D. A. Brown," made the observation that the White Star liner *Titanic*, then gearing up for its maiden voyage, was a "pitiable rowboat that ought not to be allowed to set sail, lest it be an embarrassment to these shores." Whether she had gone prophetic or dotty, it is impossible to say.

Buck Naked

To be *buck naked* today means to be totally unclothed. But that image distorts the original meaning, which was the literal one: naked as a buck. *Buck* was Appalachian frontier slang for a young Indian male, and such males, in the early contact period, typically dressed in loincloths and mocassins. Thus to be *buck naked* meant to have one's genitals and feet—but only one's genitals and feet—covered. To settlers who carried a flintlock in one hand and a Bible in the other, of course, this was morally equivalent to being nude, and so the somewhat exaggerated association of Indian youths with nudity was born.

Bulls and Bears

The stock market terms *bullish* and *bearish*, which refer respectively to an active, optimistic market and a slow, cautious one, have nothing to do with the supposed aggressiveness of bulls or the sluggishness of hibernating bears. In the eighteenth-century London stock exchange, trading notices were posted each day on a large cork pinboard (the precursor of today's electronic "big board"). These notices were called bulletins, or "bulls"; so, if the board were plastered with notices at the end of a heavy trading day, those present would speak of the "bull-ish" trend. If the volume had been light, on the other hand, the pinboard would be relatively notice-free, or bare; and they would speak of "bare-ish" activity.

Bullshit

It is a little known fact that the manure of adult bulls and oxen has a lower phosphate content than that of cows and calves. The reason for this is not clear, although theorists agree that it has something to do with the fact that cows metabolize phosphates more quickly than bulls and more slowly than their young. One zoologist, B. O. Vine of Montana State University, even speculates that the retention of phosphates in the bull may trigger his notorious aggressiveness. "Cross-species studies on this possibility," he writes in *Cud Quarterly*, "may help explain the riddle of war."

Whatever the reason, the varying phosphate contents of manures make calf manure the most desirable as fertilizer, with cow manure a fairly close second, and bull manure the poorest of all. Therefore, purchasers of manure typically pay a premium when the load is certified as coming from cows or calves. If the fields treated with such a load do not yield well, the supplier may be suspected of selling them bull manure rather than the specified product. Hence *bullshit* as a general metaphor for anything fake or misrepresented. For reasons that are not clear to me, the vernacular has not picked up the cowman's equivalent expression of praise, "That is calfshit."

Bum Steer

In the madcap 1920s, when pilots like Charles Lindbergh were making their reputations by barnstorming from air show to air

show, a lunatic fringe of young aviators was drawing capacity crowds with displays of aerial acrobatics: Their death-defying acts included wing walking, upside-down flying, and the briefly popular *bum steer*. In the *bum steer*, the pilot would unstrap himself from his seat, kneel or stand facing the tail of the plane, and manage the controls literally with the seat of his pants; that is, he would steer with his "bum." Since this feat could only be fully appreciated up close, bum steerers had to fly fairly close to the ground, and since pulling up on the controls was a difficult maneuver, the crash ratio for the trick was pretty high. Bum steering as a phenomenon soon faded, but the expression remained: To give someone a *bum steer* is to send him on the same blind, careening course that the daredevil pilots had taken.

Bum's Rush

To be given the *bum's rush* is to be hastened out the door of
restaurant or other establishment, by force or insult or both
spite of its ostensible meaning—the *rush* given an unw
PANHANDLER—the term's actual derivation is not obvious.
a misspelling of Baum. The original bum's rush was
rush," given to those patrons of French chef Leon
Paris restaurant whom the proprietor deemed un

fare. Baum opened his establishment, modestly called Chez Baum, on the Right Bank in 1887, and during the Paris Exposition two years later experienced his first wave of American and British tourists, whom he called collectively *la canaille atlantique*, or "the Atlantic rabble." The fifth in a line of distinguished hoteliers, Baum had no patience with culinary ignorance, and was known to have ejected diners from his premises for ordering inappropriate wines. Such impetuosity was rare, however, and usually the nouveau riche but untutored diner in Baum's place would be treated to general smugness and hurried service—a combination which has not entirely disappeared from Paris restaurants even today and which was known at the time as *la brusquerie baumesque*. It was this phrase that was translated as "Baum's rush."

Bunt

Unlike his cousin Mathilda Burns Bunte (inventor of the misspelled Bundt cake pan), bush league shortstop Harvey Murchison Bunte, a member of the old Kansas City Slavers, has been forgotten by history. Yet the batting technique he devised completely revitalized the national game in the second decade of this century, when the European war was drawing many fans' attention away from the diamond and toward the trenches. "Harvey Bunte," one baseball historian has said, "gave the game new life. He wasn't much of a shortstop, but he gave us baseball's forward pass."

Necessity's maternal instincts have been exaggerated, but she was the mother of Harvey's invention. In a 1913 game with New York, he had broken both his elbows after tripping over second base. Since the Slavers were without a second string, Harvey came up with two techniques that were suitable for a man in double casts. One was the now obsolete "scoop" method of fielding grounders. The other was the famous batting technique that allowed him to connect with the pitch without having to

bend his damaged joints. In his first time up with the casts, Harvey's *bunting* technique so astonished the other team that they spent precious seconds wrinkling their foreheads while he rounded the bases for a triple. The sacrifice *bunt* only came in much later.

Burn the Candle at Both Ends

To *burn the candle at both ends* means to stay up half the night, at work or play. Squab suggests, reasonably enough, that the "ends" referred to here are the last hours of daylight and darkness, but there is also a more literal explanation. In European mourning since ancient times, it was customary to "wake" or "watch" with the dead through the night, both to provide comfort to the family and to guard the body from nocturnal demons. Since

demons feared firelight, candles were burned during this vigil, sometimes in a protective circle around the corpse, but more commonly—since beeswax was expensive—at the head and foot of the coffin. Thus the *ends* originally associated with keeping late hours were the two ends of the bier.

Butter Someone Up

This synonym for "flatter" reached the West just before World War I, thanks to the 1904 British invasion of Tibet. One of the novelties that Sir Francis Younghusband's soldiers discovered there was the traditional Tibetan butter lamp, a Himalayan version of the whale-oil lamp which used melted yak butter for fuel. Because of the shortage of wood around Lhasa, this peculiar type of burning oil had a value it might otherwise have lacked; as a result, tubs of yak butter had long been prized as presents among the natives. The material success of a wedding feast, for example, could be measured by the number of butter tubs that the couple received as gifts, and the Tibetan catchphrase *na-nga-gudbe* ("only one tub") was a standard expression of disdain. So to *butter someone up* (the Tibetan is *marme-mönlam*, or "fill his butter lamps") was to ingratiate yourself with a person by showering him with gifts of butter fuel.

The British never quite got this picture. Jethro Dey (Naga Chepu), an American-born lama who witnessed the 1904 invasion, wrote in his autobiography *Under Dhaulagiri* that "Younghusband's 'butter' was British commonwealth status, and like the Romans before him he could never understand why the barbarians he had graced with his presence were reluctant to be flattered into subjection. Had he presented the High Lama with a hundred butter tubs, His Majesty's legions might have enjoyed greater success."

On the Button

The "button" you connect with when you hit something *on the button* is actually a metal disk a little larger than a silver dollar. Until relatively recently, you would find this item in traveling carnival midways: It would be attached to the end of the lever that operated the chair tilt mechanism of dunking games; hitting this button with a pitched ball would send the chair sitter into the drink. Because of the small size of the button, however, it was fairly difficult to accomplish this feat, and in this century carnival owners gradually increased the size to make the game seem more attractive. Today's "buttons" may be six or eight inches in diameter.

Cahoots

The Kahouti were an outlaw band in northern India that flourished in the heyday of British rule. Staunchly opposed to European imperialism, they were at the same time religious pacifists, and their attacks on the hegemony of Victoria's armies took the form of twitting rather than carnage. They would disrupt train lines, for example, by burning effigies of the queen on the tracks; they would place huge orders for the hottest curry seasonings and have them delivered, C.O.D., to regimental barracks. Perhaps most aggravating of all, they would volunteer as army laundry room assistants (out of love for the "Great White Mother Queen") and infest piles of clean laundry with tiny insects which they had carried inside in spice jars. Thus to be "in the Kahouti" was to be a member of a secret, hostile alliance; and to be afflicted with "Kahouti's presents" (later simply *cooties*) was to have your clothing crawling with bedbugs and fleas.

Carried Away

Today the injunction "Don't get *carried away*" is a mere social warning: The implication is that the person so warned is, through exuberance or vehemence, offending against conversational etiquette. But in the Irish countryside, where the expression originated, it once had a far graver meaning. For all their garrulousness, the Irish used to take a very guarded view of verbal arguments. As animated as a poteen-inspired quarrel might become, rough language and especially blasphemy were strictly forbidden, and there was a superstitious as well as social rationale for this rule. Bad language could bring down divine retribution on the spot—although, curiously, not from God Himself. In an interesting fusion of Christian and pagan beliefs, it was said that the blasphemer would be transported by the faery folk to their woodland realm, where he could no longer offend common decency. Thus to be *carried away* was, originally, not the fact but the consequence of intemperate speech.

Cart Before the Horse

The obvious implication of this phrase—that only an illogical person would have a horse push rather than pull a cart—was not the original one. The expression first appeared in 1889, after the Oklahoma land rush. At high noon on April 22 of that year, the government opened up to white settlers all those lands that had not yet been assigned to Indian peoples, and a horse race for the best lots ensued. The principle of lot selection was the simple one of first come, first served, but many homesteaders were not satisfied with that arrangement. Sneaking into the open country hours and even days before the starting gun, many of them were already fully settled when the fastest horses arrived. Riders who had beaten the pack only to discover that the cheaters had beaten them gave us two expressions to remember them by. One was the contemptuous designation "Sooner," which modern Oklahomans, smiling at its origin, proudly apply to themselves. The other was *cart before the horse*—an indication that the underhanded early arrivals had got in their WHOLE KIT AND CABOODLE (carts and fences included) before ever getting on a horse. Evan Barnard, who had ridden legally that day, remarked ruefully on the *cart before the horse* bunch. "We cowpunchers," he said, "were soon enough to get many of the best claims in Oklahoma, but we were not as fast as the men who had good gardens and onions six inches high that had been raised in fifty minutes."

Cat Got Your Tongue

This curious metaphor for reticence has an equally curious, and quite distasteful, background. Among the Saracens of the eleventh and twelfth centuries, as among some of their Arab descendants today, punishments were often made to fit the crime in a literal and brutal fashion. Hence the penalty for stealing was losing a hand, and for adultery it was sometimes castration. The Crusaders who made war on the Saracens learned that the most common punishment for blasphemy—misuse of Allah's gift of speech—was to have the tongue torn from the mouth. The fact that it was then sometimes fed to household pets struck the delicate Europeans as amusing, and they came up with *cat got your tongue* as a description first of the victims of this barbarity, then of mutes, and finally of quiet people in general.

Cat's Pajamas

I don't know who makes pajamas for the STARS today, but in Regency England it was E. B. Katz. The most famous of the Savile Row tailors in his day, he counted among his clients a dozen peers of the realm; the kingdom's preeminent fashion plate, Beau Brummell; and Brummell's "fat friend," the Prince of Wales. A specialist in elegant men's nightwear, Katz was known as a stickler for detail; for the pajamas of his aristocratic clients, he would use nothing but the rarest Chinese silk, and he is said to have employed two dozen seamstresses at one time to do the brocade work on one of the Prince's smoking gowns. Thus "Katz pajamas" became a byword for sartorial, and then general, excellence; the corruption to *cat's* apparently arose as a jibe among reform-minded members of Parliament.

Katz was a brilliant tailor but a poor judge of political winds. When Brummell and the Prince had their famous falling out, he continued to make nightwear for the Beau. This cost him the royal patronage, most of his noble clientele, and eventually his business. He retired around 1815 to Surrey, where his success had bought him a farm and where, evidently, he went a bit dotty. In Surrey slang "Katz pajamas" means "crazy," from a local story that in his declining years, the tailor-farmer lived day and night in pajamas. He died after falling from a horse, and Surrey legend attributes the accident to his eccentricity: Evidently he had ridden to hounds barefoot and stirrupless, dressed only in his slippery silk namesakes.

Charley Horse

Because England's King Charles II kept numerous buxom royal mistresses, his subjects jokingly referred to women's breasts as "charlies." By extension, "charley" became a slang term for milk, and a *charley horse* was a dray who pulled a milk wagon. Given the irregularity of London's cobblestoned streets, the weight of such wagons, and the general insensitivity of milk drivers to equine comfort, it is not surprising that many "charley horses" went lame, or that the expression *charley horsing* became a Restoration synonym for limping. The muscle knotting that causes temporary lameness in athletes has been called a *charley horse* since about 1750 because of the similarity of this affliction to that of the old-time milk drays.

Cheapskate

The *People's Almanac* says that New Jersey heiress Hetty Green (1835–1916) was in her day "the wealthiest woman in the U.S.— and perhaps the world." It also suggests that much of her approximately $100 million fortune was made possible by "miserliness of a truly incredible degree." She lived in a rickety Hoboken flat, for example; she dressed in what any other woman of her class would have considered mere rags; and when her son's knee became infected, she adamantly refused to pay for treatment, until eventually the boy lost a leg. As outrageous as her behavior was, however, it was outdone by that of her sister Catherine, known to her friends as Cheap Kate. Kate Robinson (Robinson was the sisters' maiden name) inherited rather less money from her parents than Hetty did, and she had none of

Hetty's entrepreneurial zeal. So, while Hetty multiplied her $10 million inheritance tenfold, Kate took her $5 million and sat on it. Literally. She too lived in a cold-water flat, and after she died in 1920, it was discovered that her bedding and her furniture were stuffed with bills, the smallest of them portraits of Ben Franklin. Out of her original bequest, only about $5,000 was missing—which meant that between 1862, when her parents died, and 1920 she had lived on about eighty dollars a year.

No one is quite sure how she did it, although documentary records make it clear that she was phenomenally stingy with beggars, and that her electricity was never turned on. Nancy Milieu's *Hoboken Weirdos*, an odd little product of the 1970s' oral history revival, supposes that Kate, like her sister, depended on the kindness of strangers, begging her bread and her rags from folks who had no idea of who she was. "The Hoboken term *cheap as Kate*," Milieu writes, "was a tribute to the woman's rabid tightness, while a *Cheap Kate*, into the 1940s, meant someone who never picked up a check."

Cheesecake

It's fairly widely recognized among slangophiles that many turns of phrase relating to cake hark back to the black "cake walks" of Reconstruction days. In these popular walking competitions, the couple that displayed the most style was declared the winner, and often *took the cake*—that is, took home a cake as a prize. It was white observers of these "fancy strut" contests who, being unwilling or unable to compete themselves, demeaned the proceedings as "mere walking," and gave us *cakewalk* and *piece of cake* for something easy. What is seldom remembered is that these cake walks engendered rude parodies in the white community. Beginning around 1900, many small towns held weekly "cheesecake walks," in which the participants were not couples but local prostitutes, and in which the strutting was accompanied by striptease. Like dogfights and like prostitution itself, these entertainments were widely banned, with no visible effect on their popularity. The backdoor entrepreneurs who ran them presented cheesecakes to the most stylish strippers as a way of mocking the original black genre, and *cheesecake* soon came to be applied to the undressed prize-winner as well as to the prize. *Beefcake* came in much later, as a way of describing "beefy" (muscular) male dancers whose behavior paralleled that of the strippers.

Chewing the Fat

Everybody knows that Eskimos eat blubber, but nobody seems to know why. Why, indeed? Why would a people with ready access to boiled Arctic hare, salmon steak, and reindeer stew choose to plan menus around whale fat? The answer lies not in gastronomy but in sex.

Since time out of mind among these hardy folk, the great whales have been symbols of virility, and it is anything but accidental that in the more traditionally minded clans, an adolescent boy still becomes a man only after he has harpooned a whale. This kind of child-to-mighty-hunter ritual is common among traditional peoples. What is not so common is the use of the slain animal's meat (in this case, fatty meat) in a further ritual proof of manhood. Once the boy has killed the leviathan, the carcass is dragged up on shore, the boy's father carves off several large chunks, and they are presented to the youngster with the injunction: "Eat this mighty beast with your bride, and you will father five thousand hunters."

What ensues is an often lengthy seclusion ritual in which the young man and his betrothed, confined in a special hut, discuss their wedding plans while mutually devouring the fat. Since this fat-chewing ceremony is thought to be essential to the couple's fertility, they cannot be married, or engage in any sexual contact, before all of it is consumed. Thus the Eskimo expression *chewing the fat* refers to any sexually promising encounter that has not yet proceeded beyond the talking stage. It was American explorers early in this century who extended the image to refer to any long, drawn-out conversation.

The fat-chewing practice is now almost extinct, but the Eskimo tongue retains two pithy expressions that recall its earlier importance. One is the designation of an impotent male as "only a fat-chewer." The other is "The fat is in the fire," which used to indicate the most grievous of social offenses—the couple's secretly burning the fat to hasten the wedding—and now has come to mean, in the Lower Forty-Eight as well as in Alaska, the beginning of any long-anticipated event.

Chip on One's Shoulder

An enduring bit of false etymology has this expression deriving from the practice of sporting wood chips on one's shoulder as a dare to others to knock them off. As Mark Twain and others have pointed out, this was an adolescent macho game during the middle of the nineteenth century; but the practice followed the expression by many years. Ronald and Peck cite an 1811 newspaper article from the Upper Michigan peninsula indicating that "Chipwa at his shoulder" was at that time already a metaphor for aggressive display. In that extremely wild area of the country, many white travelers hired Indian bodyguards, and among the tribes that were most celebrated for providing this service were the Chippewa north of Lake Superior. To have a Chippewa warrior at your shoulder did not mean, necessarily, that you were looking for trouble; it did mean you would not shy away from it. Thus, contracted, we have *chip on one's shoulder* for a person who does not fear dissension.

Bust Someone's Chops

Mutton-chop whiskers, or simply mutton chops, were a popular form of male facial adornment in the second half of the nineteenth century. The expression "buss someone's chops" arose in the 1870s as an English comment on the continental, and especially French, custom of male friends kissing on the cheeks when meeting. The English found this bussing custom revolting, and they began to speak of "chop bussing" as a distillation of all Gallic sissiness. For an Englishman to kiss another in this manner was much more than a breach of etiquette; it was tantamount to impugning the bussed person's virility. Not surprisingly, many duels were fought over this insult. Interestingly, the vernacular transformation of the supposedly effeminate "buss" into the more appropriately violent "bust" only intensified the message of insult. It is not clear which came first: the linguistic slip from "buss" into "bust," or the practice of punching, or "busting," someone in the face as the required response to being kissed.

Poor as a Churchmouse

It used to be a tradition in English country churches for the pastor to solicit monthly donations of bread, cheese, and other foodstuffs for the support of the parish's destitute. Among the survivals of this custom are the modern plate collection for the poor, the poorbox by the church door, and the expression *poor as a churchmouse*. Each region had its own jargon for describing the recipients of parish charity. In Kent, for example, they were known as "Kent clerks" because, although they were not associated with a university, they were just as impoverished as clerks (students). In most of the northern counties, they were called "Cheshire hounds," since their support often came in the form of Cheshire cats (for English cat-eating, see SKIN A CAT). In the south, where they typically received large quantities of the region's many cheeses, they were quaintly referred to as the church's "mice." It is the southern tag that has stuck as a designation for extreme poverty.

Happy as a Clam

This is an Atlantic tidewater expression dating from the mid-1800s. The popularity of clam-digging in that area aside, it has nothing to do with the shellfish. "Clam" here is a mispronunciation of "Clem," and a "Clem," to the members of the seaboard aristocracy of that era, was an unschooled bumpkin from the Piedmont—the kind of person that we would call a RUBE. The Washington gossip sheets of the 1820s and 1830s—particularly Rivers's self-styled "cosmopolitan" weekly, *The Intelligencer*—frequently poked fun at country types. A particularly supercilious columnist of the period, one "Junius Primus," laid the groundwork for the modern expression in that paper in 1833, when he mocked the supposedly simple-minded contentment of rural folks in a series of satires on "Clem Diddleseed, Yeoman." Diddleseed displayed a Pollyanna-like ability to endure misfortunes with equanimity, and Washingtonians were soon speaking of resolute contentment as being "happy as a Clem." There was a political point to the satires, too, for Diddleseed was a stereotype of the dirt farmers who supposedly had just elected Andrew Jackson. Thus to be *happy as a clam*, according to Junius Primus and his Whig admirers, was to be taken in by the president's false promises.

Clip Joint

In a *clip joint* the customer loses his money because he is "clipped," or cheated, by the management. Today the phrase is loosely applied to any establishment in which prices are high, service is poor, or hidden charges are tacked on to the final bill. In French painter Georges de la Tour's 1621 work *The Fortune-teller*, we see the original meaning of the term. It depicts an old gypsy woman who is reading the palm of a pompous young aristocrat while one of her daughters distracts him with conversation and a second one uses tiny metal snips to remove his dangling watch from its chain. In the prewristwatch era, such "clipping" operations were common practice among thieves, and in the seventeenth century, they were most common in urban coffee houses, where tricksters like de la Tour's gypsies plied their trade: The original clip joints were these establishments.

Interestingly, the advent of "clipping" illustrates a technological innovation as well as a linguistic one. Watch chains came in around 1600, as an attempt to confound pickpockets, but the underworld rapidly responded by adopting the metal snips pictured by de la Tour. These new tools were as popular among lawbreakers as fuzzbusters and window JIMMIES are today. In a 1638 catalog of "criminalles implements" published privately at Bristol, for example, we find a trio of newly developed "chayne clypperes." "They be reddily secreted," the catalog promised, "and be parfitly mayde for to part pompouse yong aristocratts from theyre bawbels."

Cloud Nine

The last third of the nineteenth century saw the publication of numerous utopian novels, most of them written by social reformers who were appalled at the depradations of industrial capitalism. To name only the most famous examples of the genre, there were Samuel Butler's 1872 satire *Erewhon*; Edward Bellamy's influential 1888 advertisement for state socialism, *Looking Backward*; and English socialist William Morris's 1891 *News from Nowhere*. All of these books had vast readerships in their day, but have long since ceased to be household names. The reverse was the case with *Cloud Nine*, an "anti-utopian fancy" concocted in 1894 by a staunch defender of the status quo, "J. P. Morgana."

The identity of Morgana has never been determined. Some literary historians believe the author was financier J. P. Morgan himself in drag disguise; others point to one Flora McDonald, the purported mistress of both John D. Rockefeller and Henry Clay Frick; still others spot a capitalist P.R. mind at work, and claim that Morgana was "a mere smokescreen for the press boys of U.S. Steel." Whatever his or her identity, it's clear that Morgana's book did provide ammunition for the enemies of social reform. The society sketched in *Cloud Nine* was an unrealistic one in which the supposed dreams of utopian socialists had been brought, finally, to fruition. There were no poor, no hungry, and no classes. Everyone held a management position, although there was little work to be done. The standard garb of the Cloud Niners was a flowing, angelic robe; their principal endeavor was harp-strumming. Cloud Nine was physically situated "about twenty miles straight up, above Boston," and the name of the society itself (a pun on the German *nein*, for "no") suggested the impossibility of the dream. It is from this novelistic attack on utopian schemes that we get both *cloud nine*, for impossible bliss, and the similarly derisive catchphrase *pie in the sky*: According to Morgana, on Cloud Nine every meal was dessert, and the ingredients of the meals all came free. In the words of the character Samuel Bombast (thought to be a parody of Samuel Gompers), "Here we toil not, nor do we spin; but every day brings us pie in the sky."

Cloud Nine enjoyed a brief vogue, especially in Boston, up until the end of the century. Andrew Carnegie thought enough of it to request that a copy of it be on the shelves before the opening of each of his newly funded libraries. Harvard radical Alexander Yarrowville expressed the common opinion of the other side in a scathing review in *Notes and Queries*: "If books could be tried for breach of reason," he wrote, "this one would be burned at the stake."

Cock and Bull Story

The usual explanation of this phrase is that *cock* refers to a boastful rooster and that *bull* is the short form of BULLSHIT. This reasonable guess is not correct. The expression arose in the 1720s to describe that particular genre of low humor in which a gullible person is involved in a "conversation" which is prearranged to make him look like a fool. A modern example is the exchange in which the victim is asked to pronounce several Scottish names beginning with "Mac" ("How do you say M-a-c-d-o-u-g-a-l?") and ends up saying "MacHine" for the word *machine*. This joke form was known as a "cock and pull story" by analogy to the firing of a pistol. The set-up conversation "cocked" the fun, and the punch line was the trigger, or "pull." Hence "cock and pull"—and then, after a printer's error, *cock and bull*—for a story that is not what it seems.

Cold Feet

Cold feet signifies timidity or cowardice not because of any logical, physical connection but because cold is the opposite of hot, and heat has been associated with bravery for centuries. The Latin verb *fervere*, from which we get "fervor" and "fervent," means basically to be boiling hot, but the extended meanings in imperial times included to be excited and to be, like a boiling liquid, in rapid motion. A Roman soldier with hot feet (*pedibus cum ferventibus*) was inflamed with the passion of battle, or as the younger Pliny might have put it, *ab pilo ad pedem*, or "from top to toe": Everything about him, from his flushed face to his impatient feet, signified his eagerness to do battle. One who lacked this excitement, on the other hand, would have entered the fray *pedibus cum frigidis*, or literally "with *cold feet*."

Cold Fish

When we say that someone with a limp, unresponsive handshake has a grip like a *cold fish*, we are being more literal than we know. In the first two decades of the eighteenth century, when English practical joking was at fever pitch, many jokesters concealed small fish in their palms with which to greet unsuspecting well-wishers. Guy Smiley refers to this charming practice fleetingly in his *Hoaxes, Jokeses, and Eye Pokeses*, calling it "the icthyologic forerunner of the hand buzzer." Naturally, the practice generated apprehension and, among those who were particularly loath to have their hands swatted with dead herring, a certain degree of restraint. By the process which linguists call transformational grammar, eventually the recipients of *cold fish* handshakes came to be called *cold fish* themselves. Since these unfortunates were often understandably wary of further casual contact, the expression became associated with reserve: By 1739, according to Squab, a *cold fish* was "a stiff, unfeeling person." (For more on the street humor of the 1720s, see HAND SOMEONE A LINE.)

Until the Cows Come Home

To wait *until the cows come home* is to wait virtually forever, that is, for an event that will never happen. The construction seems somewhat inept, for on any farm that is kept running smoothly, pastured cows are brought into the barn every night; indeed, as the great Balkanist Appleton Balki points out in a recent letter to this author, the Miposian term for six o'clock in the evening translates literally as "the hour when the cows come home." The expression means "forever" in American English because of the prevalence of rustling on our frontier. When a rancher had lost his cows to cattle thieves, he knew that their brands would soon be changed, and the opportunity for retrieving them greatly reduced. In most cases, unless he actually caught the rustlers in the act, it was unlikely that the stolen cows would ever be seen again. Hence the scoffing frontier expression for improbability: "when the cows come home and lizards fly."

Take a Crack

Take a crack, for "make an attempt," is an American baseball expression, referring to the sound of the bat as it connects with the ball. Similar phrases from the 1920s, which do not today enjoy as wide a usage, are *take a swipe* and *take a swing*. It's interesting that *crack* should have proved the most durable of the three, since it is, strictly speaking, the least accurate, in its anticipation of the hit. You can safely claim that you will take a swing, but you cannot promise the crack until after the deed is done.

Crackers

The obvious explanation of why *crackers* should mean "mad" is that the term refers to a "cracked" head. A more obscure explanation is to be recommended, however, because of its historical precision. The first usage of *crackers* in its current sense, according to Fetch and Tarry, may be traced to seventeenth-century Blackpool, the Lancashire port which figured so prominently in Britain's maritime expansion; the first to be designated *crackers* were merchant sailors. Naval historian T. V. Ajelut speculates that this may have had less to do with the city's suspicion of the transient tar population than with dockside outbreaks of ergotism, a toxic condition brought about by the ingestion of tainted grain foods. Dry crackers, or "ship's biscuits," he points out, were a staple of seventeenth-century naval stores, and at a time when food preservation techniques were minimally understood, these stores might easily have been contaminated by such natural "additives" as the ergot-bearing fungus—which has the same effect on the body as lysergic acid diethylamide, or LSD. So the sailors identifed as *crackers* might actually have been England's first acidheads.

Ajelut's theory, which appears in his history of the British navy *When the Sun Never Set*, is farfetched but not unique. In recent years historians have attempted to explain such differently "cracked" phenomena as Salem witchcraft and Van Gogh's "visionary" painting by invoking the same ergotic origin.

Up the Creek

Being *up the creek,* especially "without a paddle," is an image of extreme duress or hopelessness. This seems inappropriate, because with or without a paddle, you can easily enough escape being stuck *up* a creek simply by drifting with the current; being "down the creek" would seem a better metaphor. Squab says the explanation for this apparent error in the idiom is that the original creek referred to was one Shedd's Creek in West Virginia, which flows north to empty into the Ohio. Being "up Shedd's Creek" meant being "up" or north on the map, close to the suction of the larger stream, and therefore stuck if you wanted to go "down," or upstream.

Get it? Neither did many non-West Virginians in the 1880s, when the expression arose. That is why, so says Squab, the original form of *Shedd's* creek was transformed into the modern scatological version, so that we now speak of being "up Shit's Creek." I have to agree with Squab, since my search for an original Shit's or Shit Creek has yielded nothing. The closest I find, in Louis Stall's authoritative *Dirty Place Name Guide* (the recently revised, twenty-fifth edition) is a Shite Pond somewhere on Long Island. Stall claims the name persisted until the 1850s, when it was changed, but—coyly—he does not say to what.

Crocodile Tears

The usual explanation of this metaphor for insincerity is that "certain African tribes" believe the crocodile waters its victims with its tears to make them more tender before devouring them. No African would be so stupid as to believe that, unless he had never seen a crocodile, and it is a tribute to the persistence of racist attitudes that the story is still being told today (see, for example, the juvenile version in Karl Skatterly's *What the Bushman Believes*).

The real reason we speak of *crocodile tears* is that the Congo-based crocodile clan, of the Batuso tribe, weep ritually over their victims as a way of "righting the cosmos" after a successful battle. Radcliffe-Brown reported many examples of ritual weeping among the Andaman Islanders two generations ago. Although the Batuso as of yet have had no scribe of equivalent skill or credentials, their weeping customs have been frequently reported in the anthropological literature, especially in *African Folklore Studies,* most recently by Yale's Stukey Flowers. In his 1983 monograph "Tears for Fears," he sensibly rejects the traditional view that crocodiles—reptilian or human—cry to ridicule or deceive their victims. "Crocodile clan crying" he explains, "is a kind of existential balance wheel. Batuso elders have told me many times that if they did not cry after killing their enemies, the gods would think they were not grateful for the victory. Weeping shows humility and respect, and it hints at the sense of common humanity, common frailty, common mortality, that the crocodiles share with other clans, and indeed with all peoples of the forest. When a crocodile warrior weeps over his victim, he is saying, 'One day I know I shall join you.' The *last* thing the custom signifies is insincerity."

As the Crow Flies

Folk wisdom notwithstanding, crows are no more likely than any other birds are to fly in a straight line; their typical flight pattern, like that of most other scavengers and virtually all predators, is a widening spiral known as a gyre. They adopt that pattern, rather than the mythical line, because it more efficiently covers ground— an important consideration when you're hungry. Our expression *as the crow flies*, meaning "straight," comes to us courtesy of the Sioux and Cheyenne, who used it to taunt their traditional enemies, the Crows. In their own language the Crows called themselves *Absoraka*, or "bird people," but this was not the reason they were taunted. It was because, more than any of the other Plains tribes, they cooperated with the U.S. Army as scouts and interpreters, and so were seen by other Indians as retreating—that is, as flying "straight" away from the warrior's duties.

Actually, this charge was ill-founded. The Crows were not less courageous then other Indian groups—only more opportunistic. It is perhaps not surprising that the site of the Little Bighorn battle, where the Sioux and Cheyenne wiped out Custer, is now a Crow reservation.

Eat Crow

Two facts about traditional kinship systems explain this unusual way of saying "show humility." First, the members of most clans in tribal societies trace their lineages back to a common animal ancestor; and second, it is generally forbidden for a person to eat his clan totem, except on special occasions. Thus a deer clan member can eat salmon but not deer, and the reverse is true for the salmon clan. The idea of eating crow arose among the four-clan Paiute Indians of the American Southwest, as what anthropologists call an "ergonomic management strategy."

The tribe inhabited the arid Great Basin region of what is now Utah and Nevada, and in times of exceptional dryness it would have been virtually impossible for the tribe to maintain its strength if it had adhered to the traditional totem-abstinence structure. So that structure was modified. To the original four clans (antelope, coyote, rattlesnake, and eagle), the Paiutes added a pseudo-clan, the crow clan, in which any member of the tribe could claim membership on an ad hoc basis. This strategy instantly increased the types of food available to individual hunters, since everyone could now go after not only the other three clans' totem animals, but his own as well. When food was short, for example, a coyote clan hunter could kill and eat coyote simply by declaring himself to be a crow. The genius of the system was also a Paiute joke: There *were* no crows in the Great Basin. So an ad hoc crow gave nothing up.

But there was a psychological down side. By becoming a crow to stave off hunger, a person automatically forfeited membership in his original birth clan—and this involved a lowering of tribal status. When mountain men observed Paiutes during famines, they noticed that all the members of the tribe seemed dejected and embarrassed. When asked to explain this, they invariably responded, "We must eat like the crow." Thus "eat *like* a crow" was the original metaphor for being humble; *eat crow* was a mountain men's variant.

Ronald and Peck have suggested that "eat like a crow" suggested the bird's own manner of consumption: For a person to be as unparticular about his food as this scavenger meant that he had little self-esteem. This attractive idea breaks down on the basis of chronology. As just mentioned, crows did not inhabit the Great Basin in aboriginal times; that is precisely why the

ingenious Paiutes chose them as the fifth clan totem. The first actual crows reached the region some time in the 1820s, as pets of the mountain men themselves. The story of their introduction from northern Mexico is admirably told in mountain man José Cuervo's *Journal of Thirteen Dry Seasons*, published for the first time in 1981 in Arroyo University's "Dusty Papers" series.

Have a Crush

"Crush" in this phrase is a distortion of the French word *crèche*, meaning "crib." To be "in a *crèche*," or to "have one's own *crèche*," in seventeenth-century France, meant you were so smitten with love that you were as helpless and irresponsible as an infant. The expression was made popular by François Souche, an uninspired contemporary of Racine whose dull tragedy *Hero and Leander* nevertheless enjoyed great success in the Paris of the 1680s. In this retelling of the ancient legend, the Greek youth Leander is called *crèché*, or "crib bound," because he is incapacitated by his passion for the priestess Hero. She is a bit of a tease, and when Leander drowns on his way to their rendezvous, Souche has a handmaiden describe the tragedy as a *vol de crèche humide et terrible*, or "a fearful and wet theft of the crib." This ugly phrase, truncated in translation, gave us the expression *robbing the cradle*, which initially meant "toying with one's affections," and gradually came to be applied more precisely to an older lover trifling with a younger. The current May–December connotation, without the negative implication, came into use around 1750.

Cry in Your Beer

The original of this was *cry in your bier*. In eighteenth-century England, effusively sentimental persons were often ridiculed as being "gushers" (hence *gushy*) or "pumps" (from which, indirectly, we get *drip*). To accuse someone of being likely to cry in his bier was the ultimate rebuke: It meant he was so prone to whimpering that even death could not stop his tear ducts. We use a similar hyperbole today when we speak of a perenially tardy person as being "late to his own funeral." That expression also comes from the eighteenth century, as does a quite charming one that we have forgotten. In Jocelyn Squeeks's diary for the year 1754, we read this comment on an irrepressibly jovial acquaintance: "Squire Kenworthy is the verry soule of whimsy. He will lead the dance upon his owne grave." "Dance the grave" and "lead the dance" were popular contemporary expressions for good humor.

Currying Favor

To *curry* the favor of a superior is to seek that person's good graces, often ostentatiously or obsequiously. Such toadying is older than the species, of course, but the first favor-seekers to add *curry* to the recipe were the stableboys of Louis XIV. The Sun King was extremely fond of the mounts which he housed at his palace in Versailles, and to ingratiate themselves with their sovereign, his grooms curried the poor beasts around the clock; thus, even if the king should pay a midnight visit to the stables, he would find the animals actively attended. Paddock slang for this quite unnecessary labor was *l'etrillacion en Sa faveur*, or "the currying into His Majesty's favor."

Give a Damn

The original phrasing was "give a dam" or, more precisely, "give a tinker's dam." Tinkers were the traveling Mr. Fixits of merrie olde England (and merrie olde Scotland and Ireland). Since they flourished before the advent of mass production, they typically made their own tools or had them made to order by blacksmith friends. Each tinker had his own idiosyncratic designs, and the unfamiliarity of tinkers' tools among the general population gave rise to the slang terms *thingamajig* and *whatchamacallit* to describe any implement of obscure function. But virtually every tinker had his dams. These were small metal wedges or shims which the handymen used to pry, brace, or *jimmy* recalcitrant machinery, and which they carried with them, in various sizes, by the hundreds. So common were these tiny items on tinkers' workbenches that they became a byword for insignificance, as in the eighteenth-century phrase "not worth a dam" and the nineteenth-century addition "give a dam." *Dam* thus served the same metaphoric purpose as *straw* and *fig* did among farmers, and as *farthing* did with financiers. The spelling *damn*, meaning "curse," suggests not the insignificance of swearing (that was serious business among the tinkers) but the orthographic capriciousness of the time.

Dark Horse

It's little known among the general public that, other things being equal, dark horses run faster than light ones (this is why you never see a palomino at Churchill Downs). On the Texas frontier in the 1870s, impromptu horse races were a daily diversion, and the owner of a spirited, fast mount could augment his income considerably by betting against strangers in pick-up races. It was not uncommon for equestrian hustlers to daub their roans and blacks with whitewash, so that they resembled such slower strains as the Appaloosa and the bay. Experienced racers could spot the deception in an instant, but newcomers were often fooled, as the "light-skinned" frauds proved surprising winners. Thus we speak of an unexpectedly successful political candidate as a *dark horse.* The practice also gave us the expression *show one's true colors*: This is exactly what would happen after a heated run, when the whitewash would be streaked by the horse's sweat.

Deadbeat

This is a corruption of "debt beat," which is itself a contraction of "debt beater." To "beat a debt" in colonial America was to avoid paying it through quasi-legal means: either by declaring bankruptcy or, more frequently (since the bankruptcy courts could be sticklish), by physically leaving the colony in which the debt was contracted. It is from this popular debtors' strategem that we get not only *deadbeat*, but also the command *Beat it*, for "Leave."

Traditional etymologies are therefore wrong when they claim that being *dead beat* means being completely (that is, "dead") insolvent (that is, "beat," or BROKE). Many colonists who had successfully beaten their debts by emigration went on to become prosperous citizens. The modern connotation of the term, as referring to HOBOES or PANHANDLERS, dates from about 1700, and can be traced to New York, the then still tiny city which was experiencing a population surge thanks to the influx of "debt beaters" from Connecticut and New Jersey. The New Yorkers considered the new arrivals little better than common tramps; but ironically, in saddling them with the newly debased sense of *deadbeat*, they were disguising their own origins: The most prosperous of these New Yorkers had begun their careers by fleeing from their obligations to European masters.

Dime a Dozen

One of the more obscure forms of Buddhist meditation practiced in traditional Japan was known as Daimdu Zen. *Daimdu* literally means "bent nail," but it is more generally applied to any small, insignificant object. Members of the Daimdu school, centered in isolated Kita Iwo, would kneel for hours or even days in meditation, their eyes fixed intently on a bent nail, in order to attain what their founder, the sixteenth-century monk Subaru Toyota, described as "the supreme knowledge of the small"—that is, the understanding that the least significant of material objects was still capable of releasing one's "Buddha nature." The subtlety of this concept was lost on the American merchant sailors who followed Commodore Perry into Japan. To them, "dimduzen" meant merely an appreciation of trifles. The punning expression *dime a dozen* was invented around 1860 to ridicule not only the "bent nail" concept but Oriental mysticism in general: To those intent on opening up the East to capitalist enterprise, nails and holy men were equally common—and equally worthless.

Dingbat

Archie Bunker would no doubt be surprised to learn that the *dingbat* (his pet name for his wife, Edith) was a precursor of the slapstick. The slapstick was an actual stick (technically, two sticks fastened together) which produced a loud "whacking" sound when it connected with the butt of a joke on the tent circuit and vaudeville theater stages; we get our designation *slapstick* for farcical comedy from the popularity of this device. It was only invented in 1811, however, by a Munich theater manager named Dieter Schauspiel, who marketed it in Europe as a *Klapschtick.* Before Schauspiel, the standard mock weapon of the comic stage had been the Italian *bastone di buffone*, literally "bat of the buffoon." This was a small, light stick modeled after Punch's club in the commedia del l'arte, and was used not only in sham fighting but also to ring the bell for the curtain. The "dinging" sound of the bell led to the English expression, first used around 1780 in this country. Its appropriation by *All in the Family* had nothing to do with the original meaning; it was used, evidently, because both *ding* and *bat* in English carry suggestions of mental incapacity.

Dodge the Issue

The *Oxford English Dictionary* gives the source of the sixteenth-century verb *dodge* as "unascertainable." Thanks to the recently discovered Ryall Manuscript, written in Henry VIII's hand, we can now ascertain it quite clearly. I quote from Professor Skeeter Davis's discussion of this valuable find, published last year in *Tudor Tidbits*:

"As part of his assault on English monasticism, Henry in 1536 engaged a number of royal investigators and charged them to search for 'irregularities harmefull to the Crowne' in the monasteries' accounts. Abbots, naturally resentful of this intrusion, refused admittance to these hirelings, arguing on a perfectly sound legal footing that the king had no sovereignty over their affairs. One investigator, however—whom Henry identifies only as 'oure good Dodge'—refused to be repulsed by 'monkish logic.' Dodge must have had casuistical training, for he was in many cases able to overcome the abbots' objections 'by taking theyre protests as but gossamere, and nimbly making the case for the Kinge.' Exactly what techniques Dodge used to redefine what was a thoroughly clear-cut issue, Henry does not say. He does say that the man was highly successful—'he hath broughte his Kinge eight hundred of pounds in this single monthe'—and that in the future he will instruct all his investigators, when they 'bee obstructed by monkish sophistries,' to do 'as this worthy hath done, and Dodge it.' Thus to Henry's subjects a glib, tendentious argument—especially one that waltzed around the facts—was spoken of as a "Dodge of the issue." The wider sense of *dodge* soon followed."

A Dog's Life

As that intrepid amateur ethnologist, Lady India Dove-Nolen, pointed out in her memoir *Dayaks and Kayaks*, we associate a "doglike" existence with misery not because of canine deprivation, but because the Dorg caste of the Afghani foothills are among the most despised of the world's despised minorities. Thought to have emigrated from somewhere in the Himalayas several hundred years ago, the Dorgs practice a primitive form of nature worship which makes them outcasts among the Muslim population, and which long ago forced them to take up residence in the arid and aptly named Zereh Depression. There, as Dove-Nolen described them, they "spend their days digging for lizards, praying for the rain that never comes, and attempting to secure sustenance from the occasional traveler in exchange for a handful of their 'sacred' sand." Their marginal condition made "a Dorg's life" proverbial, by about the early 1800s, for extreme poverty, and also gave rise to the catchphrases "sick as a Dorg" ("There is no word for health in their language," Lady Dove-Nolen wrote) and "go to the Dorgs," as an Afghani equivalent of "go to hell." With the 1898 publication of Dove-Nolen's book in England, all these expressions came into vogue, but it was barely a generation later that *Dorg* became corrupted into *dog*, and the original meanings were forgotten.

Doozy

This slang term for something remarkable or exceptional at one time was spelled *deucey*, and the old spelling gives a clue to its origin. Twos, or "deuces," are the most common wild cards in poker playing, so for something to strike you as "deucey" meant it gave you as much satisfaction as a deuce in the hand would give a gambler. The term arose in the South in the 1890s. Its association with the Duesenberg luxury AUTOMOBILE was a later, tendentious invention: The automobile's manufacturer, Frederick S. Duesenberg, adopted the expression in his company's advertising not because it was a contraction of his family name, but because it was a generic term of high praise. As Professor Pierce B. Arrow shows in his entertaining history *From Horseless Carriage to Ottomobile,* the so-called father of the *Doozy* car was actually born Frederick S. Grossrad. He changed his name to Duesenberg in 1821, and invented the contraction two years later.

Inside Dope

In the intrigue-ridden days before World War I, all the major (and most of the minor) European powers kept spies in each other's capitals, to gather up-to-date information about shifting alliances. The *inside dope* in those days was not the information that was gathered, but the person doing the gathering. Then as now, governments favored inconspicuous and nonthreatening agents. Among the most highly prized of these professionals were men and women who could pass themselves off as being deaf mutes; often these "insignificant" people, posing as house servants or tradespeople, were able to secure closely guarded information because others were not aware that they could hear it.

Each government had its own jargon for these "silent" spies. The Germans called theirs the *Taubstummbrigade*, or "deaf and dumb brigade." The French spoke of *maîtres de la surdité*, or "masters of deafness." The English expressions were *dummy* and *dope*, both of them vernacular terms for the deaf. Information gained from an "inside dummy" or *inside dope* was generally considered highly reliable, and gradually the sense of the "dope" being credible came to be attached to the information itself. At the same time, to get the *straight dope* meant to get information that was as clear, or "straight," as that which you might get from one of these supposedly speechless informers: *Straight dope* is a vestige of the World War I catchphrase "as straight as an inside dope's tongue."

Dork

In contemporary teenage slang, a *dork* is a socially inept nonentity; the term has the same general connotation as *nerd* and the earlier *square*. But while both those terms are native insults, *dork* comes to us by way of Germany. The German verb *durch-*

eilen means "to hurry," or to pass over something, or someone, in haste; *Durch* was a slang contraction of *Durcheiler*, or "hurrier," that was originally applied to bureaucratic officials who seemed too busy to attend properly to their clients. By the process that Heinrich Giffelgach calls "denominational transmogrification," the word eventually came to be applied to the person being passed over, rather than the one doing the passing; thus a *Durch*, and among German-Americans a *dork*, came to mean anyone unworthy of consideration.

Giffelgach's theory is explained in a none-too-lucid monograph with the misleadingly sprightly title "DT: A New Approach to the Old Switcheroo." It appeared in the Spring 1978 issue of *Modern Language Knots*, and created an instant *guerre des feuilletons* between DTers and their detractors (whom Giffelgach calls DDTers). Interested readers may want to consult that journal for details on what Giffelgach calls "the *Ursinne* of such argotic conundrums as why the person taking the journey should be called the *Fahrt* (!)." A knowledge of all the European languages would be helpful, although familiarity with German, Frisian, and Basque is sufficient.

Get the Drop on Someone

This expression recalls the gunfights of the Old West. In the classic Hollywood versions of those sagebrush confrontations, the Bad Guy and the Good Guy face each other from opposite ends of a dusty street, the Bad Guy goes for his six-gun, the Good Guy beats him to the draw, and another town is made safe for democracy. It all happens so fast that the novice Western fan may miss the fine points. These were outlined ably in 1882, in an anonymous pamphlet called *The Gunman's Guide to Glory*, published by the Boot Hill Preservation Committee of "Billy the Kid's home town"—Brooklyn, New York. According to the author

of this pamphlet, the "Perfect Killing" consists of five steps. In (1) the Hover, your gun hand "floats above the revolver hilt like a hummingbird." In (2) the Drop, your hand drops "ever so naturally but, oh yes, ever so fast" to the gun. In (3) the Draw and Cock, you extract the gun fluidly from the holster while at the same time cocking the hammer with your thumb. In (4) the Aim, you "get the dirty varmint in your sights." And in (5) the Shoot, you "send him where he belongs—straight to Hell." From this description it should be obvious that no matter how good a shot a gunman might be, he might still end up in Hell himself unless he was quicker than his opponent beginning with step 2. This is why *getting the drop right* became the gunfighter's equivalent to the boxer's *beating him to the punch* and the runner's *beating him out of the blocks.*

In actual practice, of course, the formalized directions given in this and other duelists' guides were often ignored in the interests of expediency. A high number, perhaps the majority, of Western gunfights did not take place face-to-face in the street, but from behind packing crates and shattered windows. The modern negative sense of the expression arose because so many glory-seekers *got the drop on* the backs rather than the fronts of their rivals. Thus, although it is technically inaccurate, many armchair desperadoes will speak of Robert Ford as having *gotten the drop on* Jesse James.

Down in the Dumps

Bouder in French means "to sulk," and a *boudoir*—in spite of its lubricious connotations—is a place where a person may retire to pout; the modern sense arose because this place was usually an anteroom off milady's bedchamber. In Spanish, the equivalent is *dompa*, a vernacular abbreviation of *dompedro*, or "morning glory." During the reign of Ferdinand and Isabella, when a person got into a snit, he or she would retire not to an antechamber, but to a garden; and, since morning glories were all the rage in that period, the flip command *Vaya a las dompas*, or "Go to the morning glories," was frequently addressed to a pouter who needed some time to work things out. Contemporary English pouters, following the Iberian example, were told to go to the "domps." Eventually a visibly depressed person was spoken of as "already in the domps."

Probably the value of sitting in a garden was its own soothing reward, but at least one social historian feels there was more to the *dompas* than this. Noting that morning-glory seeds were ingested by hippies in the 1960s as a way of inducing psychedelic visions, Professor T. F. "Natso" Leery of the Los Angeles-based Guru Connection claims that Spanish courtiers may have sought the same experience. "It can hardly be accidental," he wrote in *Cranial Explosion Quarterly*, "that the Castilian *dompa* fad peaked under Joanna the Mad, or that the most imaginative of Iberian mystics, Teresa of Ávila, wrote her works at the same time. We know that these women had gardens. Why doubt they had access to seeds?"

Ear to the Ground

It's frequently stated that the American Indians were the first to put their ears literally to the ground, in order to listen for approaching horses. This explanation is only half accurate. Yes, the Indians did adopt this posture, but it was not to listen for hoofbeats. In his entertaining memoir of life among the Comanche in the 1850s, Texas trapper Nolen Hunter explains the custom as a ritualized questioning of the earth itself. "Tree That Walks and other old scouts always told me they was listening to the heartbeat of their mother. It was the earth herself giving them the news. Sometimes they'd ask a question right out, and sometimes it would be about an enemy's horses. But sometimes it would be about the weather, or what the squaws ought to cook up for dinner. Laughing Grass told me he got the best damn chili recipe in all of Texas from asking the earth 'How much comino?' That old story about listening for the horses is something they worked up for the greenhorns. Amazing what them fellers will believe. Tree That Walks and me took one of them out along the Brazos one day. Tree That Walks puts his ear to the ground and raises up and points south. 'Fourteen hooves,' he says. 'Coming this way. Two days' ride. Palomino in the lead.' You shoulda seen that greenhorn taking notes."

Easy Street

Eduardo "Cool Eddie" Zabaglione was a genial con man who made a fortune in Florida real estate at the turn of the century. When his customers discovered that the plots they had bought were a mile offshore and a mile down, Eddie was forced to relocate. He came to New York with his money, and doubled it in an ice cream emporium where he sold something that he called zabaglione, but that in fact was frozen milk with chopped nuts. With the proceeds from this fake zabaglione, Eddie constructed a palazzo-style mansion in the heart of what is now Little Italy. His high living there became legendary, and the street where the mansion sat became known first as Eduardo Zabaglione Street and then as E. Z. Street. By homonymic corruption, *easy street* became a synonym for great wealth.

The suggestion by certain gastronomes that Cool Eddie invented zabaglione, and named it after himself, is nonsense. In his amusing memoir *How I Fleeced the Four Million*, he admits that he named himself after the ice cream, not vice versa: "I was born and raised little Freddy Mertz."

Eavesdrop

In intrigue-ridden Renaissance Italy, political spies were nearly as numerous as assassins, and one method by which these functionaries gathered information gave us our term *eavesdrop*. If the hired listener of the Borgia clan wished to get the INSIDE DOPE on the latest scheme of the Corleone faction, he might climb onto the roof of the Corleone villa and lean his head over the edge near a window to listen in, or *eavesdrop* on their plans. This rather insidious, not to mention dangerous, tactic is reflected in the modern Italian expression for eavesdropping, *ascoltare presso la finestra*, or "listening at the window," and in the now obsolete warning *Il tetto possede orecchios*, or "The roof has ears."

Lay an Egg

The idea of failing by *laying an egg* dates from the fifteenth century, when the English upper classes were adopting the French sport of tennis. Scorekeeping in those days was done on a large slate at mid-court, and the French love of balance specified that the slate indicate a score for both players, even if one had not yet taken a point. Thus the scorekeeper gave the scoreless player a zero, and since the figure resembled an egg, to *mettre l'oeuf*, or "lay the egg," came to stand for the accomplishment of nothing. The equation of zero and egg survives, of course, in the modern referee's call: "Thirty–Love" is the Anglicized version of the original "Trente–L'oeuf."

Egg on Your Face

To have *egg on your face* means, of course, to look foolish and embarrassed. In Portugal just after the Moorish conquest, it was considered a mark of masculine honor to be able to hurl an egg skyward and catch it in your mouth as it fell. Missing the egg, and thus ending up with a face full of albumen, marked the hurler as a lesser man—in Portuguese, an *ovolemidor*, or "licker of eggs."

The Lisbon Psychoanalytic Society, in a recent monograph on Mediterranean virility games (*ludi di macho*), calls this practice *Ovobota* ("Egg Toss"), but is not very instructive on its origin or deep meanings; the suggestion by the society's Professor Lusiad that it exemplifies "womb envy" is provocative but purely conjectural. What is known for sure is that the practice was widespread in the Iberian south and, according to some authorities, replaced cockfighting for a while in certain areas. Evidently both the game and the expression were brought to the New World by Portuguese crewmen of Columbus. Tragically, only the expression survived.

All Your Eggs in One Basket

This has nothing to do with farming. It is a steel-mill expression dating from about 1870, when the great Pittsburgh steel plants turned out thousands of tons of steel every week. At this rapid rate of production, quality control sometimes suffered, and as a result many factories produced quite high percentages of defects—warped train rails for example. In most plants, the below-par items were marked with an X, pulled from the production line, and once an hour recycled toward the smelter in large mesh baskets that ran on overhead pulley systems. Since overloading these baskets could be hazardous, a common-sense safety rule was adopted: "Don't put all your Xs in one basket."

By the turn of the century, the meaning of the phrase was transmuted, so that it served as a caution against overspecialization. Henry Ford, who at the time was specializing completely with his Model T, is reputed to have amended the injunction. "It's all right to put all your Xs in one basket," he told a critic of his single product line. "Just watch that basket."

One Over the Eight

At male drinking parties in ancient Rome, it was a custom for the guests to toast each other's mistresses, taking one goblet of wine for each letter of the honored damsel's name. Thus the longer the name, the more inebriated the toasters would become. By consensus, women's names of seven or eight letters—Juliana, for example, or Anapesta—were taken as the appropriate toasting limit. Should Sextus's mistress have a name longer than that, it was considered wise, in the interests of fairness if not sobriety, for him to allow an abbreviated toast; the company might drink to Pertia, for example, rather than the complete Propertia. But

Sextus was not obliged to FUDGE the rules, and if he wanted his friends to drink to all nine letters of Propertia's name, he could insist that they do so. In that case they would be downing goblets *ultra octo*, or "beyond the eight." This is why *one over the eight* has come to stand for drinking beyond one's capacity.

Eighty-Six

The lunchroom counter expression *eighty-six*, meaning "We're out of it," derives distantly from the nautical term *deep six,* meaning to send someone six fathoms deep, or to kill him, and more immediately from a CIA directive. The directive was issued first in the 1950s, and although it has since been expunged from agency records, its memory lives on in CIA folklore. In the words of my personal inside snitch: "Number 86 was part of the old code book, giving detailed directions to field operatives. You've heard of the expression 'terminate with extreme prejudice'? You learned how to do that in Number 86, so it became a slang term, in the 1960s I think, for putting somebody out of it or for saying he was already out of it. You know: 'Where's Joe?' 'Oh, he's been *eighty-sixed*.' Damned if I know how that leaked."

English

English is the eccentric spin that a billiard player puts on a ball by hitting it slightly off center. Now a term of approval (as in, "The guy's got great *English*"), it was originally contemptuous. When billiards were invented in the sixteenth century, the first great champions were French. They lost their lead in the following century to their cousins across the Channel. Basing their shooting techniques on Newton's recently published laws of motion, English players rapidly outstripped the French masters, who, in spite of evidence to the contrary, remained committed to the proposition that a struck ball always follows a straight line. One sports historian has called this stubbornness "the ultimate perversion of Descartes's conviction in *clair et distinct* ideas." It was the English players' willingness to "tease" their billiard balls into slightly elliptical paths that gave them the lead in international competition, and that made "Anglais" a term of resentment. To *English* a ball, among the French, meant to slice it unfairly—and to win.

Even Steven

This expression for equity or fairness goes back to an obscure British monarch, the tenth-century Saxon king Stephen the Greedy. To bolster the kingdom's defenses (and, his critics said, to line his own pockets), Stephen instituted a series of revenue-raising practices that were as ingenious as they were absurd. He collected usage taxes on public improvements before those improvements had ever been made, so that his people paid bridge tolls for the privilege of walking through water, and park taxes for acres of briar. He introduced a concept called the Air Tax, by which families paid a daily fee per head for the right to breathe "theyr Sovereyn's Aire." And, in the innovation by which he is remembered, he provided a twist on the old marital custom by which a lord could share the bed of his vassal's bride even before the vassal himself had done so. This was known as the *jus primae noctis*, or "right of the first night," and in most cases the right was suspended, with the vassal handing over a fee in lieu of his wife. Never one to miss a financial opportunity, Stephen collected this fee at every marriage, since technically everyone in the kingdom was his vassal; and in addition he created the *jus secundae noctis*, or "right of the second night," by which all bridegrooms in the kingdom were charged a fee for sleeping with Stephen's queen, the Frisian Princess Siuletta. They had to pay this second-night fee whether or not they embraced the custom, for, in the wording of the Saxon chronicle, "It bee not the Kinge's culpabilitie iff that the brydgroome chuse not the banquette; it hath ben prepared all the same to his expense."

For her part, Siuletta seemed not to resent this arrangement, and is even said to have commanded compliance in certain cases—whether out of a sense of fairness, or lust, cannot be said. In any event, the reign of this odd couple gave us two enduring expressions. Stephen was known even in his own day as "Even Stephen," because his "second night" rule offset the first. His queen's name became the Norman *Siulet*, and was shortened eventually to *slut*.

Go to Extremes

Any etymological dictionary will tell you that the word *extremes* means "out of bounds," and that it comes ultimately from Latin *ex termine* by way of Old French *ex termes*. What the dictionary will not mention is that, in Provence during the early Middle Ages, Extermes (sometimes spelled Aix Tremes) was a place—or rather a number of places. Few Provence villages in those days had money enough to support a jail, and fewer still had reason to build one. But petty thieves, disorderly drunks, and other troublemakers had to be punished somewhere, so villages set up temporary "banishment regions" just beyond the outskirts of town. These were unfenced but clearly designated areas (similar to minimum security prisons) in which transgressors remained on their honor until their terms of confinement were completed. Since these holding areas were all outside of town, they became known collectively as *regions ex termes,* and to *go to extremes* (in the Languedoc dialect, *vaz aix tremes*) meant you had committed a crime that would merit your temporary isolation.

Face the Music

This expression dates from World War I, when the rhythmic rat-tat-tat of machine-gun fire was known, in a grimly humorous phrase, as "barrel music." The barrel referred to was obviously that of a gun, although there may also have been a connection to the tapping and grinding sounds of the barrel organ. Whatever the origin, to *face the music* meant to go over the top of the trenches, into the quite unmusical atmosphere of No Man's Land.

Fat Cat

The original *fat cat* was not a billionaire industrialist but a cat dressed to look like one. He was the rotund feline villain of the 1890s cartoon strip *Micetown Follies*, which was drawn by Chicago anarchist Francis "Red" Tulane as a running attack on American capitalism. The heroes of the piece, which was set in the fictional factory town of Micetown, were the rodent family of Biff and Muffy Mouse. Like the human workers of that era, they had to contend with such normal indignities as twelve-hour workdays, cramped housing (they lived in a company-owned packing crate), and reliance on the bosses for their food (they received a weekly bread and water allowance, and half a pound of cheese at Christmastime). The factory owner was Fat Cat himself, whom Tulane depicted as the stereotypical nineteenth-century robber baron, showing nothing but contempt for his laborers. Sporting a sizable paunch and a velvet vest, a top hat and a cigar, Fat Cat was fond of quoting tycoons, and had an unerring instinct for remembering their least enlightened comments. It was from Fat Cat's mouth, for example, that many Americans first heard John D. Rockefeller's humble observation, "God gave me my money."

Tulane ran his strip in the Chicago dailies, where it was a cult favorite with radicals and warmly hated by business leaders. He successfully defended himself against lawsuits by several regressive industrialists, and was only driven out of circulation when he took on the government as well as business. That was in 1898, when he had his hero Biff describe the then-popular Spanish–American War as "Fat Cat's cronies playing pool—and using our bodies as the balls."

Fiddling Around

Several English expressions link violin playing with frivolity. *Fiddling around* means fooling around, and three related terms—

fiddlesticks, *fiddle-faddle*, and Scarlett O'Hara's pet dismissal, *fiddle-dee-dee*—all mean, roughly, "nonsense." The association arose not with regard to today's four-stringed instrument, which is far too sensitive to respond to mere *fiddling around*, but to a fourteenth-century precursor, the single-stringed *viol des genoux,* or "lap viol." The typical lap viol was only about fifteen inches long. Laid flat on the lap like a dulcimer, it was played by stopping the single string with the left thumb while hitting it over the soundhole either with a small stick (hence *fiddlesticks*) or with a diminutive paddle (hence "fiddle-paddle," later corrupted into *fiddle-faddle*).

In his amusing history of obsolete instruments *Où Sont Les Saqueboutes d'Antan?* ("Where Are the Sackbuts of Yesteryear?"), Alsatian musicologist Andrew Owen says that the sound produced by the lap viol was "a cross between a penny whistle and a tortured cat." For this reason, and because it was "too boring to play, even for children," it passed out of favor around 1500, leaving only a linguistic legacy.

Flapjack

The origin of this synonym for "pancake" is explained in cowboy Rance Bozeman's *Trail Gossip*, published by the Drygulch Historical Society in 1894 and reissued in 1948 in Arizona State University's "Great Western Liars" series. I quote from this unjustly forgotten memoir:

"Most folks don't know it was Jack O'Malley gave us the moniker *flapjack*. Jack was a cook on the Goodnight Loving runs in the '70s, and he was the worst damn trail cook in the business. Keno Williams claims Jack invented bobwire stew *and* moose turd pie. I dunno about that, but I can tell you he turned out pancakes that made saddle leather taste real good. We called 'em "Jack's flaps" and that got twisted around to *flapjacks* by some turkey-brain newspaper feller. It was *flaps*, you see, because you could hold 'em up in a dust storm and they'd flap like a mill vane in the wind. The good Lord ain't yet made the cyclone could break one of them sumbitches in half. Keno says he flung one out of camp once and it busted a rattlesnake's spine. Keno stretches, of course, but I'll tell you the God's honest truth. If it wasn't for them flaps of O'Malley, this good ol' boy could chew solid food."

Fleece

The verb *fleece* in the sense of "to cheat" sounds as if it refers simply to the act of shearing, or fleecing, a sheep: A criminal's victim may be deprived of his money or goods just as the animal is deprived of its wool. Actually, the term originated among British travelers to the Balkans in the early eighteenth century, and it refers to a con game of the time. Many of the travelers, educated in the classics, were familiar with the story of Jason and the Golden Fleece. Taking advantage of their knowledge and their gullibility, Greek sharpers would dye ordinary sheepskins yellow and sell swatches of them to the British as remnants of the mythological relic. It is not clear how many of the buyers really believed they were getting gold, and how many purchased the hide fragments as mere curiosities or souvenirs; what is sure is that hundreds of these "golden" curios ended up in British parlors, and for a time even enjoyed a certain vogue as antimacassars. Johann Flügelschinken, in his entertaining history of hoaxes *Homo Stupens*, suggests that during the period when the Grand Tour was an essential part of the British gentleman's education, there were probably as many pieces of the Golden Fleece in British homes as there had been pieces of the True Cross in medieval Europe: "Jason's ram proved even more profitable to the sons of Hermes than the Brooklyn Bridge would prove to their descendants."

Fly-by-Night

It is commonly assumed that *fly-by-night*, used as a synonym for "unreliable," dates from the early days of aviation, when unlicensed pilots would transport contraband—and the occasional reckless passenger—by night to avoid the authorities. Not so. The term appears for the first time in 1894, in Aurora Welles's popular memoir *Epigraphia Americana, or My Life Among the Rustic Pedants.* The book related the author's experiences as secretary to the English antiquarian Fishbottom McH. Forbes-Hamilton in their 1872 journey throughout the United States, and the expression appears as part of a diatribe against medicine shows delivered by the scholar to his scribe. "These villainous enterprises, my dear Miss Welles, are the very spirit of the abrasive. They resemble nothing so much as a fly by night, incessantly buzzing and tapping upon one's peace and then, when one has finally seized the infernal switch, most conspicuously and mysteriously gone." Hence the nineteenth-century use of the phrase to describe anything fleeting or insubstantial.

Welles, a one-time schoolteacher and a minor expert on the Augustan Age, saw herself quite consciously as the Boswell to Forbes-Hamilton's Dr. Johnson. In the preface to her chatty history, she admitted that her employer always had "greater wit than pith," but claimed that in the backwoods America of the 1870s, he was still, by comparison with other crackerbarrel philosophers, a "veritable Hercules among the pygmies," and "as quick as an adder with a retort." It was his sharp tongue that eventually did him in. During a particularly virulent exchange of bon mots somewhere north of Baltimore, a local poetaster challenged him to swim the Chesapeake "as Leander had swum the Hellespont," and he was drowned for his effort. Welles, in a last lugubrious chapter, notes that the Baltimore daily paper, to which Forbes-Hamilton had sent numerous letters denouncing American mores, announced his passing with a retaliatory headline: "Fishbottom Fishes Bottom."

Fly Off the Handle

This curious synonym for "lose control" started as the name of a kitchen game (*Küchenspiel*) played by German immigrants in the Philadelphia area in the latter half of the nineteenth century. Participants would catch relatively sedate insects—ladybugs and other beetles were the favorites—place them on the handle of a pot of water, light the burner, and lay bets as to when the heat would make them *fly off the handle*. At the turn of the century, the city's Teuton League and other pan-German groups claimed that this somewhat barbaric entertainment was the invention of gypsy, not German, immigrants, but the claim was discredited in 1967 by the Romany linguist Tesla Gavotte. Working with a huge cadre of gypsy volunteers, Gavotte scoured the Philadelphia newspapers for the period 1885–1900, and proved conclusively that the earliest mentions of the game were in the punning German form *Henkelfliege*, or "handle fly."

Foggy-Minded

It is purely coincidental that this phrase suggests a mind filled with fog. The original nineteenth-century expression was "fogey-minded," and it comes from the name of the same English eccentric who gave us the designation *old fogey*. His full name was William P Fogarty, and a quick idea of his oddity may be gained from the fact that the self-chosen P of his name, like the parentally chosen S of Harry Truman's, stood for nothing at all. Fogarty was an itinerant merchant who peddled everything from sawdust to eels throughout the south of England in the 1850s. Virtually everything he tried to sell was without value, and he was only able to sustain himself on the charity of people who thought him mad. Dressed in a flop hat and tatterdemalion military uniforms, he dispensed simplistic folk wisdom along with his wares, so that he became known variously throughout the south counties as "the sage of Surrey" and "the basil of Brighton." Among his more famous bits of advice to potential customers, as recorded in numerous folk stories, was that given to a young Falmer woman who wished to know the meaning of life. "Eat when you are hungry," he told her, "and when you are tired, lie down."

Fogarty might have remained only a local phenomenon had it not been for Oxford's Lewis Carroll. The famous poem which Alice recites to the caterpillar in *Alice's Adventures in Wonderland*—the one which begins, "You are old, Father William"—is commonly taken to be a parody of Robert Southey's doggerel *Old Man's Comforts*. In fact it is a portrait from life of the man Oxonians called "the witless wonder," whom Carroll met while vacationing in Brighton. Carroll himself often admitted that this so-called parody was really a *poème à clef*, and although he was too sly to say so in his lifetime, it is clear from the penultimate stanza that Fogarty was the model for "Father William." "You balanced an eel on the end of your nose," Carroll wrote; this trick was Fogarty's signature.

Foot in One's Mouth

In China before the British invasions of the nineteenth century, the person of the Emperor was considered so sacred that his subjects could not even mention it—that is, they could not audibly refer to his physical being—without incurring penalties. Among the more whimsical of these penalties was the public penance known as *ch'in n'idz wai-peng*, literally "as tactless as a newborn baby." The person who had been so rash as to imply that the Emperor had a corporeal as well as spiritual presence (perhaps by uttering some innocent comment about how well he looked that day) would be taken by armed guards to a central square, stripped of all his clothing except a diaperlike loincloth, and have one of his feet yanked upward and forced into his mouth. There it would be tied for several hours, to the great amusement—not to mention civic education—of passersby.

The British soldiers who witnessed this punishment in the 1850s probably did not understand its quirky logic. As the Chinese term for the practice makes clear, its intent was to demonstrate the true—that is, infantile—nature of the offender by putting him into a physical position that usually only infants can achieve. The British did understand that it was the penalty for transgressing the Chinese laws governing conversation, and so they quite correctly brought the expression *foot in one's mouth* back to England as a metaphor for conversational blunders.

Foot the Bill

Contrary to the opinion of many authorities, including the usually careful *Oxford English Dictionary*, this expression does not reflect the custom of signing one's name as a promise of payment at the bottom, or foot, of a bill; the Romans were *footing their bills* fifteen hundred years before that custom arose. The expression is really a botched translation of the Latin term *foederem facere syngraphae.* Literally, this means to make (*facere*) an agreement (*foedus*) about a promissory note (*syngrapha*). When a Roman debtor agreed to pay a creditor in the future, he put the evidence of that agreement—either a signature or a seal—on a parchment outlining the terms, and this evidence was sometimes spoken of as the agreement, or *foedus,* itself. In Roman Britain *foedus* became *foed,* and was ultimately corrupted into *foot,* while the other two terms of the Latin formula were, more accurately, simply translated: *facere* became "make" and *syngrapha* "bill." Thus in a second-century record of the Witangemot (see MAD AS A WET HEN), we read that Bodo, a farmer, is granted a one-year loan of seed from the assembly, "to the wich he this daye foeds the bill."

Forty Winks

The expression *catch forty winks*, for "to take a brief rest or nap," recalls the career of one of Europe's most enterprising eccentrics, the Danish spiritualist Niels Müdegaard. Born in Copenhagen around 1870, Müdegaard remained there for almost fifty years, working obscurely as a civil servant, until in 1919 he experienced what he later described as "a conversation with the Lord of Death himself." This lord, whose name Müdegaard gave as Trixie, informed him that the "realm of the departed" had gotten over-crowded owing to the slaughter of World War I, and that no more entrants could be admitted until renovations were completed in about two decades. It was to be Müdegaard's mission to teach people how to live longer, and he would do this by training them in exercises to retard the aging process.

Armed with a "tablet of instructions" which he said Trixie had provided, Müdegaard left Copenhagen for Paris, and set up the first of many "clubs" in which "members only" could acquire his novel teachings. "Müdegaardism" became enormously chic, with spiritualists and public figures alike flocking to attend demonstration lectures on such mysteries as "Sitting as an Aerobic Activity" and "The Retention of Saliva for Better Health." By the mid-1920s there were Müdegaardists in every major European capital, and franchises reaching as far west as Los Angeles.

Most of Müdegaard/Trixie's techniques were obvious variations on yogic breathing exercises, but one was unique and phenomenally popular. This was the so-called Forty Winks Pattern. According to the Dane, an enormous amount of body energy is lost—"wasted beyond recall" was his phrase—each day through involuntary blinking. People could add hours to their life expectancy every day, he claimed, if they learned to regulate their blinking so that in any given hour they would blink (or wink) no more than forty times. As difficult as this exercise sounds, it was

attempted by thousands of disciples—many of whom, Müdegaard claimed, "recaptured vast reservoirs of inner strength by thus developing their Eyelid Power." It was because the pattern supposedly promoted restfulness that we associate *forty winks* with napping.

In 1928 Müdegaard returned to Copenhagen, where he lived peacefully until his death ten years later. In his biography of this bizarre teacher, *Trixie's Bulldog*, H. V. Fechten notes that Müdegaard died happily. "A week before his demise he wrote to the city paper, announcing that a world war would begin within a year. He was gratified, he said, that his life's work had bought Trixie some time to get ready."

Worn to a Frazzle

Woven cloth has since very primitive times consisted of a warp and a woof, and the warp, or foundation, of the cloth has usually been made of stronger stuff than the crosswise "filler," or woof. In Anglo-Saxon times, the material used for the warp was an extremely durable "yarn" that was formed not exclusively of wool, but also of the "binding" stems of reedy plants, which would be added to the wool during spinning. The Saxon word for "reed" is *frazol*. So for a cloth to be "worn down to the *frazol*" meant that the woof was nearly gone, and that the garment was about to fall apart.

Freeloader

In group drinking in British pubs, an unwritten rule governs payment: One person volunteers to buy the first round, a second one volunteers for the second, and so on until the circle is completed and it is again the initial buyer's turn. A person who accepts drinks from his mates but leaves the pub before his turn is due is called a "pint-shyer" in the north and a "free-loader" in the south. Such a shirker is always "shy" his pint of beer, and has gotten drunk, or "loaded," for free.

Freudian Slip

It is a little known fact that a distant cousin of Sigmund, one Theophrastus Bombastus Freud of the Munich Freuds, was the real originator of the term *Freudian slip*. A lacemaker by profession, Th. B. Freud, capitalizing on the lubricious interest aroused in the German population around 1900 in the theories of his Viennese cousin, produced a line of lacy lingerie that left far less to the imagination than *The Interpretation of Dreams* had provided it. Among the most popular items in this naughty-nighty collection was a diaphanous shift that became known, far beyond Munich, as the *Freudisches Unterkleid*. Basically this means "Freudian undergarment," although in his advertising Th. B. made full use of the happy accident that *Freud* in German means "joy." When the garment was marketed in Britain, it became the "Freudian petticoat" and then the *Freudian slip*. It was quite by accident that *slip*, with its other meaning, became the English translation of Sigmund's *lapsi linguae*, that is, "slidings of the tongue."

The Munich Freuds, incidentally, stopped speaking to the Vienna Freuds in 1905, right around the time that Sigmund's idea of a slip was on everybody's tongue and when, coincidentally, sales of the Unterkleid were falling off. The Munich clan felt, understandably, that Sigmund had stolen their thunder and made a reputation on their expression. In the Munich municipal archives there is an unfinished Freud family history by Fr. Aphrodite Freud, the granddaughter of the wronged Theophrastus. She concludes a bitter chapter on the *Unterkleid* episode with this comment: "Uncle Siggy was always a copycat. If it had not been for Grandpapa Theo, he would never have developed his dirty mind."

Frog in One's Throat

Hoarseness or garbled speech owing to laryngeal congestion is known as a "frog" in the throat not because of any supposed resemblance of such speech to amphibian croaking, but because, to the English, it sounds like French. The often noted French fondness for *grenouilles* has made them "frog eaters" and "frogs" to the English since the end of the eighteenth century; the language itself has been known as "Frog" since the early part of this century. To have a "Frog in one's throat," therefore, means to speak like a Frenchman—specifically, with the, uvular *r* that is the *pons asinorum* of students of French. The vernacular link to throat clearing is expressed in the Victorian insult, "If you can gargle, you can speak French."

The Germans share the English bias, and the expression; they too speak of having a *frog in the throat* (*Frosch im Hals*). The French themselves, in retaliation, long ago adopted the expression "have a cat in the throat" (*chat dans la gorge*) for the same physical condition. This is an obvious chiding reference to the eighteenth-century English mania for cat stew (see SKIN A CAT).

Fuddy-Duddy

This slang phrase for a person who is old, pointlessly meticulous, and/or generally ineffectual is a mispronunciation of the Italian *futi-tutti*, a Neapolitan contraction of the more proper *futile tutti*, meaning "totally useless." It came into being during the Renaissance, when it was commonly applied to aging courtiers and government functionaries, although Vitelloni, with his usual capacious attitude toward the *verbo offensivo*, also recommends it as a sexual insult. (See also VITTLES.)

Fudge

To disguise the pings and knocks of an aging automobile, dishonest car salesmen in the 1930s would sometimes "mask" the engine or axle assembly before showing the car to a buyer. This could be done in a variety of ways, but the most common was to pack the rattling joints or pistons with a sticky substance, both to hold them together and to deaden the sounds. The three most commonly used substances were chewing gum, putty, and chocolate fudge. When chewing gum was used, it was said to *gum up the works*. The use of putty led to cartoonists' onomatopoeic transliteration of an old motor's sound as *putt-putt*. The use of fudge gave us, simply, *fudge*, for "doctor the evidence" or "cheat."

The fascinating story of the fudge game is told in B. Lou Reddy's miscellany *The Chocolate Front End and Other Horrors*, just published by Broken Door Press. Gum and putty had been used exclusively through most of the decade, Reddy says, and fudge came in just before the war, to fool increasingly savvy buyers. Being dark, it could not be detected easily against a background of mechanical grime; and, since it melted soon after the purchase, it left no evidence of the ruse. Thus con artists adopted it widely: It is Reddy's opinion that, of the approximately 20,000 pounds of Swiss chocolate that were imported into this country in 1939, "no less than ten percent was eaten by ball joints."

Gaga

This synonym for "crazy" is vaudeville slang, dating from around 1900. In those days no less than today, the pressures of life on the road, combined with the financial instability of show business, often took a mental toll on traveling acts. For psychological reasons that are beyond the scope of this book, comics seemed to suffer most in this regard: The "burn out" rate among gag men, according to a contemporary statistician, was "no less than 51.3 percent higher than the average." In referring to this phenomenon, outsiders often spoke of "stage shock," but the performers themselves had different names. Morris Bernstein, the "Buck" of the popular comedy duo Buck and Doe, noted in his autobiography *Yucks for Yokels*, "When a silk-tights-and-doublet lad went around the bend, we called him 'Ophelia-ed up' or 'Leary.' When one of us yucksters started dreaming of fruitcake, we said he'd been 'gagged out' or 'ga-ga-ed.' Also, when the house was going nutsy—when it was one of those nights when you can't lose, when you could read a laundry list and keep 'em crying—we'd say that the audience was *gaga*. Jimmy Durante used to say that you couldn't buy a house with that spunk, and let me tell you, I knew him when."

Take a Gander

As a slang term for "look," *gander* dates from the German occupation of France during World War II. Vichy headquarters in many towns were kept strictly off limits to the locals, for fear that a casual "passerby" might relay overheard Nazi plans to the Re-

sistance. But wandering livestock, especially in the smaller villages, could hardly be so easily curtailed, and Free French sympathizers took advantage of this fact to create a unique espionage system. Taping the recently invented miniature tape recorders under the wings of a duck or a gander, they would send the animal in the direction of the town hall and, when it returned, send the taped information on to the Resistance. The practice was discovered only in the summer of 1943, when overconfident members of the Jura district Maquis taped small cameras to birds' beaks to secure visual information. The Gestapo quickly discovered this innovation, hanged the perpetrators *and* the geese, and invented the phrase *werfen einen Gänserichblick auf*, or "throw a gander's look at," to describe any illegal observation. After the liberation of southern France, this was translated and shortened by Allied soldiers to the current English expression.

Down the Garden Path

The London district of Tyburn, now called Marylebone, was the site of medieval public executions, and "Tyburn tree," until the eighteenth century, was a slang term for the gallows. Just north of Tyburn was The Garden—an expanse of shrub mazes that lay adjacent to Hampstead Heath and that, in 1684, the city council had turned into a French-style horticultural showpiece. The showpiece had an odd pragmatic value in that it offered criminals about to be hanged a last-minute possibility of reprieve. In addition to the usual hangman's fee that all the condemned had to pay, they could pay an extra two shillings for the privilege of "trying The Garden." If they had the money and the inclination to do this, they would be led blindfolded into the maze, the blindfold would be taken off, and they would be given one hour to find a path to the Heath. Once on the Heath they were free; if after the hour they were still lost, they would be found and led out to their deaths.

One might have expected all condemned criminals to try this last resort, but in fact very few did, for it was widely believed that the so-called path did not exist. The Garden had been constructed during the tenure of the notorious "hanging mayor" Royford Beame. Knowing this, and realizing that no person who paid the two shillings had ever been known to get his money's worth, London's criminals generally saw The Garden as a mere revenue-raising scheme. By 1700, throughout the underworld, to lead or take someone *down the garden path* had become a metaphor for deception.

Gee Whiz

This exclamation of surprise is often said to be a corruption of the name Jesus, invented to avoid the potential hazards of uttering the divinity's name too lightly. Possible, but not provable. I prefer the African origin which is given in Lord Stanley's journal—a book of enormous popularity by which, I think it likely, the expression was transported to England. Stanley calls the Congolese *jija oo idz* "one of the commonest cries of surprise and, more precisely, of incredulity. It is typically uttered in sarcasm, and may be roughly translated thus: 'Yes, the gazelle has eaten the leopard.'"

Geek

Today's *geeks*—the social undesirables of our high schools—are the linguistic descendants of the early twentieth-century carnival geek. As so poignantly depicted in the 1947 Tyrone Power film *Nightmare Alley*, a *geek* was a sideshow "monster"—typically, the carny drunk in disguise—whose "act" included such endearing feats as eating refuse offered by the crowd and biting the heads off live chickens. Like the medieval fool, the modern *geek* served to absorb and obliquely "justify" the anarchic impulses of the community: The figure provided what Tschako calls a "sponge release for social dis-ease"—the same purpose served by so-called inept adolescents today. Partridge traces the word to German *gucken*, meaning "to peep," but Tschako, more convincingly, opts for *Geck*. A *Geck* in nineteenth-century Germany was a dandy. Thus the *geek*, often dressed in a tuxedo in German carnivals, "embodied and transformed the pomposity of his tormentors; his willingness to enact the secret vices of the middle class was the Bavarian equivalent of *épatement de la bourgeoisie.*"

Get One's Goat

In eleventh-century Lapland, before they discovered the nutritional value of reindeer milk, most of the inhabitants kept goats. As has always been true among nomadic peoples, the raiding of livestock herds was common, and our expression *get one's goat*, meaning "to tease or aggravate," comes from the Old Lapp *gottegiten*, meaning "to steal." Gradually the connotation of theft widened to mean theft of honor or dignity as well as property, and *getting one's goat* came to mean robbing someone of equanimity or aplomb.

It's a relatively mild expression today, but in medieval Lapland goats were serious business, and the Lapps were far less accommodating than we are about having their goats gotten. One of their most ancient curses, rendered literally, reads, "Let it happen that the goat you have taken from my pasture eats all of your clothing in the village square." Unfortunately, the alliteration of the original is lost in this English translation.

Goldbrick

A *goldbrick* today is a shirker—someone who doesn't do his fair share. Since such a person cheats his employer and fellow workers, it's not surprising that the original meaning of the word was "swindler." A "gold brick artist," in the 1880s, was a con man who sold worthless gold-painted bricks to the ignorant, representing them as pure ingots. The scam was particularly popular in the Western gold fields and in Midwestern metropolises, like Kansas City and Chicago, where there was a greater supply of greed than common sense. To *goldbrick* a person at the time was to defraud him either of money or, if he was your employer, his time. To fall for a goldbricker's scheme was to prove yourself *thick as a brick*.

Goofy

Today we associate *goofy*, meaning "silly" or "foolish," with the floppy-eared Walt Disney character who is all heart and all thumbs. But that Goofy had a couple of ancestors. One was the

blundering comic-strip character Goofus, who with his indistin-
guishable partner Doofus entertained Chicago *Sun* readers for
about a decade at the turn of the century. Goofus and Doofus,
who were expert at such formidable tasks as walking into walls
and spilling soup in their laps, may have been the immediate
prototypes for Disney's dog. The other ancestor—and the one
from whom we originally got the adjective—was the Italian
painter Massimo Gufo, a contemporary of Andrea del Sarto whom
art critic Ian Candy has called "a deranged Florentine primitivist
who appeared either two centuries too late or five centuries before his time."

Gufo in Italian means "screech owl," and Massimo took every
opportunity to "sign" his paintings with the head of that bird.
Whether he had produced one of his characteristically pale, almost pastel, landscapes; a figure study (Candy calls his nudes
"frighteningly anticipatory of Picasso"); or one of his approximately 500 self-portraits, the owl's head would appear somewhere in the picture. This visual tic became his stylistic signature,
creating some notoriety for him throughout Italy in spite of his
quite ordinary drawing. Candy goes so far as to say that the owls
were his only distinctive feature: "Like Hirschfeld's Ninas and
Keane's bulging eyes, they made the unremarkable instantly
remarkable."

To Gufo's contemporaries, who were much enamored of the
concept of the *uomo universale*, or Renaissance man, the artist's
obsession with his own name was charming for a while, and
then suspect. Well before his death in 1525, *gufo* had become
Florentine slang for "eccentric." "This eponym," Candy writes in
Art News and Nuisance, "was adopted throughout Europe as a
time-saver. Just as Werther, centuries later, would be able to
summon up all of German classicism by uttering the single word
Klopstock, so Renaissance gentlemen of Shakespeare's time
could, without bothering to explain themselves, evoke an entire
world of unconventional behavior by smirking knowingly and
saying 'Gufo.'"

Up For Grabs

In Depression-era diners and lunchrooms, stale food or food that had fallen to the floor was seldom simply thrown away. In that hungry period it would often be put to the side for the local poor or itinerants; the more charitable restaurant owners would also provide fresh food for this purpose. Typically such donations were placed at the far, or "up," end of the lunch counter, where they could be taken at will by the first comer: hence the tramp's expression *up for grabs.*

With a Grain of Salt

This translates the Latin expression *cum grano salis*, and dates from early imperial times, when payment for goods and services was often made in the form of that rare and desirable commodity, salt; our word *salary*, in fact, comes from the Latin *salarium*, which was a salt allowance given to Roman legionnaires. In a business transaction, the Roman merchant might paradoxically "sweeten" the deal by offering a portion of salt along with the product he was selling. Since even shoddy merchandise might be made to seem more attractive with this salt inducement, taking something *cum grano salis* came to mean accepting, with a grain of suspicion, what would normally be considered unacceptable. Eventually the phrase was applied to ideas as well as commodities.

On the Gravy Train

British soldiers brought this expression back from India about a hundred years ago, seriously distorting its meaning in the process. To the Buddhists of that region, material wealth was hardly a thing to be desired, much less sought, but rather an obstacle on the path to enlightenment. The general notion was very similar to the often-suppressed Christian one: that great riches are baggage, not boon. So to be *in the gravy* or *on the gravy train* was a pun. It suggested not only that you had enough money to buy meat, but also that you were too ignorant to realize that meat-eating *and* money led to death—or, in Buddhist terms, to spiritual emptiness. Luxuriating in your material comforts, you were able to ignore what should be obvious: that you were on the train to the grave, meat and all. Naturally, this subtlety escaped the British, and so we have the modern image of the "grave train" as a kind of upwardly mobile joy ride *au jus.*

Good Grief

The apparently oxymoronic exclamation *Good grief!*—so favored by Charlie Brown of the *Peanuts* comic strip—is actually not as paradoxical as it sounds. The grief referred to is that felt by Christians at the crucifixion of Christ. Since at least the fourteenth century, the faithful have spoken of this grief as metaphysically good for the same reason that they speak of Good Friday as good—because the sadness of that day prefigures the Redemption. Behind the expression is the same logic that calls the expulsion from Eden "the paradox of the Fortunate Fall."

Grind

Grind became slang for an excessively hardworking student late in the 1850s. Yarrowville suggests that the neologism may have been related to the loosening of students' morals during the Crimean War. The term had for centuries referred to prostitutes, and university protests against the war did have an undercurrent of anti-Victorian libertinism. Yarrowville's theory is that a *grind* was originally a student's whore or kept woman, then the student himself, and finally "any bookish person." To this reasonable conjecture I would add a technological observation. The pencil sharpener was invented in 1849. Possibly *grind* came to be associated with studying because students were the most conspicuous "grinders" of the new invention.

Gut Course

A *gut course*, or simply a "gut," in American college slang is one in which you don't have to bust your guts—in which the material, the professor, or both are easy. The term came to the United States in the 1890s, on the lips of German transfer students, who like their American counterparts were attracted to easy-access learning. In German, *gut* means, simply, "good."

Hairsplitting

This synonym for excessively fine reasoning first appeared in English in 1820, in Thomas Mitchell's study *Aristophanes*. Mitchell used it to describe the activities of the student philosophers in the playwright's *The Clouds*, that satire on sophistry in which the characters address such momentous questions as whether gnats hum through their mouths or through their tails. Socrates, whom Aristophanes unfairly depicts as a divinity to these noodle-heads, was called by Mitchell "the quintessential *hairsplitter* of his time." The implication, of course, was that the philosopher was so devoted to nit-picking (see NITTY-GRITTY) that he resembled someone attempting to split a hair down its length. At the time, this was virtually impossible, but with the invention of the opticisor in 1869, it became child's play, and this caused a critic of Mitchell to remark, in *Notes and Queries*, that "if Socrates was indeed a *hairsplitter*, that only proves he was ahead of his time— just as Dr. Mitchell was surely behind his. The Mitchell approach to hair, one supposes, is to shred it with a cleaver like a cabbage." It is a comment on the influence of *Notes and Queries* that this passing snap at a deceased antiquarian generated its own *mot du jour*: a "hair-cleaver," in the 1870s, was one to whom, in Squab's word's, "all things were pretty much the same."

Half-Assed

It used to be a custom in northern Europe, when a farmer lost an animal to age or disease, to have the beast stuffed and mounted publicly, both as a sign of sentiment for the quasi-pet and as a way of showing status: If you could put a dead cow on display, rather than selling the carcass for income, you were obviously a person of means. Usually the stuffed beasts would line the owner's property, or be placed "naturally" in his wooded areas, like the artfully situated busts and statues of the *jardin anglais*. Naturally, the more stuffed beasts a farmer could afford, the greater his status, and this equation was memorialized in various phrases. A *north forty*, in the thirteenth century, was an extremely wealthy landowner—someone who could afford to stuff forty beasts in the northern half of his property alone. To be *cowed* was originally to be "out-cowed," that is, to be shown up by a neighbor with more stuffed cows. And the supposed Americanism *one-horse town* actually derives from the late medieval slight, "He hath but a one-horse establishment"—that is, only enough money to stuff one Dobbin.

With the economic crunch of the fourteenth century, fewer and fewer farmers could afford complete taxidermy, and this led to an innovation. Status-seekers who were short of cash might have only the front half of an animal stuffed and then display the beast

against a backing wall, the way modern hunters display their trophies. The resulting half-cows and half-asses were much derided by the more affluent, and the term *half-assed* arose around 1400 to describe anything done incompletely. At the same time, to "go the *whole hog*" became a byword for material success. "He doth neyther stinte nor cavill," the contemporary monk Alec of Yarrow wrote scathingly of a landowner who had stuffed a pig rather than distributing it among his serfs, "but feedes his hungrie on chaff as he goeth the wholle hog."

Hand Over Fist

To make money *hand over fist* is to accumulate it at such a rapid rate that it can barely be counted. There is a faint whiff of impropriety about the phrase, as if a person making good so fast is probably doing something illegal. It's not surprising that the expression first enjoyed wide popularity during the 1920s, when the vast fortunes made on the bull market (see BULLS AND BEARS) were so often generated by "irregular" trading. But the phrase predates that era by a hundred years. It arose among riverboat gamblers before the Civil War, when the placement of a palm over a closed fist was one of many signals between gaming partners by which they defrauded the ignorant. Two other expressions from that period which suggest deception more blatantly are *pulling one's nose* and *yanking one's chain*; the latter refers to watch chains.

My Hands Are Tied

In Roman law courts during the early Christian period, the *advocati* who had been raised in Italy were prone to extravagant gestures, as well as extravagant arguments, in the defense of their clients—so much so that *manuloquans*, or "hand speaking," came to be an early equivalent of "legalese." To cut down on the distractions offered by this flamboyant mode of address, one magistrate, a Sextus Vapnerus of Brindisium, frequently ordered lawyers' hands bound, so the case could be made *solo verbo*, or "by the words alone." To have one's hands tied, therefore, meant originally that you were inhibited in expression; only later did it pass into the vernacular as an image of impotence in general. Modern Italian, incidentally, retains the original meaning. In most of the south, and throughout Sicily, *mano legato*, or "tied hand," means inarticulate or mute. The great Italian-born bullfighter Manoletto (his name is a contraction of *mano letrado*, or "lawyer's hand") was so called because he did not speak until he was almost five years old.

Hanky-Panky

This term, meaning illicit and especially sexually illicit activity, is the English form of Italian *anca panca,* which translates literally as "hip bench." It is one of the forms of *verbo offensivo* recommended by Vitelloni (see VITTLES) in his classic insult handbook, and seems to have enjoyed a considerable vogue in the first half of the sixteenth century. Foxpaw's translation of Vitelloni gives the following explanation of the term: "When that ye shall calle a person a cuckolde to his face, it be meete and most economicalle to say simplye *hanca panca*, which is to saye, 'A hip on a bench.' The meaning of whych is to wit: that the hip of the personne's owne wyfe is upon the benche of a neybor, and that theis hip be not alone." It is a sign of the extreme volatility of Renaissance gentlemen, in England as well as in Italy, that they could evidently take this tortuous frivolity seriously. "Manye a nobil duel hath beene foght," Vitelloni announces grandly, "to defende the sleighted honour of milady's *anca.*"

Drop of a Hat

When a medieval European wanted to challenge someone to a duel, he threw his glove or gauntlet, to the ground; if the challenged party picked it up, the fight was on. In seventeenth-century Mexico, where gloves were unknown to the native peoples, macho rivals modified this custom—brought to them by contentious conquistadors—by throwing hats at each other's feet. In bare-knuckle brawls as well as in knife fights, a dropped hat (*sombrero decado*) was the signal to begin, and to be constantly looking for a dropped hat (*vigilante al sombrero*) meant you were ready for trouble: hence the modern sense of *vigilante.*

One curious twist made these *duellos de sombrero* a little safer than the "glove duels" of the Europeans. In addition to initiating the action, the dropped hats also served as protection. Each fighter's hat was considered his "home base," and if he wished to catch his breath or retreat from a knife thrust, he could gain a temporary respite by stepping on it. Ethnochoreographers generally agree that the balletic leaps and bounds that this rule imparted to the fighting were the original steps of the Mexican Hat Dance.

Hat in the Ring

Etymologists have searched in vain for a primordial ring into which political candidates were supposed to have hurled their headgear as a symbolic announcement that they were running. The reason no such ring has been discovered is that it never existed. The original ring was Vienna's fashionable *boulevard peripherique*, the Ringstrasse or "Ring Street." Campaigners for Austrian public office used to devote great attention to this street, not only because of the votes to be had there, but because it was a prime source of campaign contributions. To go *im Ring* ("into the Ring") or *um Ring* ("around the Ring") with hat in hand meant to solicit support for your campaign. In Vienna, where (as an old adage had it) the situation was "always desperate but never serious," DARK HORSE candidates were often described as *im Ring Hutschleppendere*, or "those who dragged their hats into the Ring." Brought to America by Austrian immigrants, this became the more active and sanguine expression *throw one's hat in the ring*.

Bite Someone's Head Off

This unsavory expression once referred to an even more unsavory practice. Among the Jivaro Indians of the Amazon, headshrinking is a widespread practice, and the warrior who has shrunk the heads of numerous slain enemies generally wears them as a prestigious decoration, on a braided belt. The display of such symbols of military prowess is thought to both reflect and enhance the wearer's *arutam*, or "soul power." A way of getting even more *arutam* than the headwearer is to sneak up behind him when he is sporting the belt and literally bite one of the heads off the string. A young man who is able to do this without being killed by the owner of the heads is reckoned a person of enormous soul power: a *kakaram*. Because these head-biting escapades often reflect a high degree of animosity between the parties involved, anthropologists who reported on the practice around the turn of the century helped to popularize the expression *to bite someone's head off* as a metaphor for acts of general, and then merely verbal, aggressiveness.

One of these early investigators, the Chicago ethnologist Illinois Smith, reported in his 1913 monograph "Heads Up: An Ergonomic Analysis of Cranial Ingestion" that many headowners sported their trophies not only to boast, but to taunt. "The belt of heads serves as a dare: It helps to organize and ritualize aggression in much the same manner as, for example, wood chip display did on the American frontier." (See CHIP ON ONE'S SHOULDER.)

Heebie-Jeebies

This slang term for nervousness or *the willies* comes from the Congolese Pygmy term *hiba-jiba*, which in its narrowest sense refers to physical tics and muscle spasms, but which more broadly suggests the anxiety and nervousness demonstrated by European missionaries upon their first contact with the naked forest people. A literal translation of *hiba-jiba* would be "to be outside of one's skin." Evidently the original sense of the phrase was a directly visual one: The person who was *hiba-jiba* twitched noticeably, as if discontented spirits within his body were attempting to exit through his skin. French and Belgian missionaries who introduced *the heebie-jeebies* into Europe failed to popularize the colorful image behind the term, although curiously they did popularize its opposite: in French to be *dans sa peau*, or "in one's skin," is still a metaphor for a lack of agitation, or inner contentment.

Hem and Haw

To *hem and haw* means to avoid making a point or a commitment by BEATING AROUND THE BUSH. The phrase recalls the faithful wife of Odysseus, Penelope, who promised her suitors that she would answer their proposals as soon as she finished weaving a death shroud for her aging father-in-law, Laertes. To stall them until Odysseus's return from Troy, she undid every evening what she had woven that day. The suitors were dim enough to be fooled by this ruse for ten years, and even after they finally discovered it, they were put off again by a second strategem. Penelope, having finished the garment, said she would decide among them once she had hemmed it; but again she tore out her handiwork each night. Homer called this process of dissimulation *rapsimo zerbos*, or "left-handed sewing," since Penelope would sew the hem from left to right and then rip it out from right to left. In Chapman's famous translation of the *Odyssey*, the description became *hem and haw: hem* for obvious reasons, and *haw* because it was (and still is) the standard drover's term for urging a team to the left. Had the ancient Greeks sewed in the opposite direction, Homer might have said *rapsimo dexios*, or "right-handed sewing," and our phrase for equivocation would be "hem and gee."

Heyday

A *heyday* is a period of prosperity or accomplishment. Today such a period might last years or centuries—we speak of the *heyday* of mercantilism or of the Pony Express—but in medieval England, as the name suggests, it was a rather momentous single day. Under the manorial system, serfs who worked a lord's fields throughout the year were entitled not only to the lord's military protection but also, at harvest time, to a share of the land's proceeds. Indeed, the fundamental difference between a slave and a serf was that the serf was "paid" in vegetables and grains. Among such in-kind payments was the hay which the serfs would bundle around October for the winter feeding of livestock. Their own stock had to be supplied from this fodder as well, and the day the lord set aside each year for the distribution of the serfs' share was known, appropriately, as the "hay day."

In the early Middle Ages, this day was a moveable feast, but by about 1400 custom had congealed, and November 10 had become the common date. This is why we call the night before that day *Halloween*: It was originally the evening before hay-allowance day, or "Hay Allow Even." The witches of contemporary Halloweens are vestiges of the medieval Hay Hag, a legendary field spirit who was thought to be able to frighten the lord into showing bounty. Their broomsticks and black cats are reminders of the Hag's two principal emblems. She carried a handful of hay with a stick bound into it (much like the Roman *fasces*) to beat the lord if he should prove selfish; her feline friend kept rodents from the grain.

Hick

Country people began to be called *hicks* in the first decade of this century, during the period when John Dewey's progressive, child-centered educational theories were calling into question the time-honored precepts of American learning. Among those precepts was a belief in the value of corporal punishment. Around 1900, communities beyond the reach of Dewey's influence were called "hickory towns," because teachers in them still made frequent use of the disciplinary hickory stick. Soon rural folk in general were called "hickories," and by World War I this had shrunk to *hick*. So a *hick* was originally a believer in the value of traditional education. (See also RUBE.)

High and Dry

In the Old West, the most desirable farming land was the well-drained "bottom" land near the rivers. When a new area was opened for settlement, naturally this fertile land was staked out first. Late arrivals were left with the far less desirable plots sloping up from and away from the water—land that was literally *high and dry*. Used in a general, nonagricultural sense, the expression first became popular along the Brazos River in Texas around 1860. Rance Bozeman's *Trail Gossip* contains an anecdote about an ignorant newcomer from the East who, thinking he would secure himself "the most advantageous prospect of the Plains," staked out his farm at the top of a rise. "With the Brazos snaking below him through the cut," Bozeman writes, "he was thinking 'I am High and Mighty now.' But all the poor dogey got was *high and dry*."

Hijack

During the HEYDAY of British piracy in the Caribbean, many buc-caneers were supported by the Crown. Not all, however, were so fortunate, and the poorer relations of such superstars as Henry Morgan and Francis Drake had to resort to unconventional meth-ods to reap the rewards others reaped by direct attack. One such method was to send young girls—the daughters of the pirates themselves—to commandeer anchored Spanish vessels. Typi-cally, the girls would board a ship in groups under the pretext of selling the crew food; two or three would conceal themselves below decks while the others occupied the men; when night fell, the hidden ones would emerge, surprise and knock out the night watch, and send rope ladders over the side for their fathers. The pirates would then sail the vessel out of port, often with the captain kept as hostage, and seldom with a shot being fired.

To the Spanish this insidious tactic became known contemp-tuously as *hijarismo*, from the noun *hija*, meaning "daughter." In letters sent home by outraged governors, the phrase *nos hi-jaron* ("they daughtered us") appeared frequently. When, as often happened, these letters fell into the hands of other brigands, individual pirates with imperfect Spanish read the governors' flowery script variously as *nos hijacon, nos hijarod*, or *nos hi-jaced.* Probably because this last misreading closely approxi-mately English syntax, many pirates adopted it as a kind of ep-ithet, and began referring to themselves as "hijacers."

Hillbilly

In the history of graffiti, each generation seems to have a trademark or, as a "subway artist" might put it, a tag. The most visible tag today is the California-inspired "happy face." In the 1940s it was "Kilroy," and before that it was "Billy Hill." We don't know who started the Billy Hill fad of the 1930s, any more than we know who drew the first "happy face." We do know that, until the Civilian Conservation Corps obliterated most examples, this quizzical-looking folk philosopher stared out at travelers from thousands of rest stops across the land. With his peaked mountaineer's cap, his big eyes, and his ever-present corncob pipe, Billy Hill represented the robust shabbiness of a nation fighting for survival. In the sound assessment of Wendy Babagenoush, author of *Why the Depression Failed*, the character embodied "both astonishment that the American dream could have soured, and the resilience with which the homeless met their fate."

Billy Hill's fusion of surprise, disappointment, and good humor was expressed not only visually, but in the "Letters to Mr. Roosevelt" that accompanied the drawings. In a typical example from Missouri, the writer praises the president's National Recovery Administration (NRA), but suggests that the letters ought to stand for "Nobody Receives Anything." Other alphabet organizations were similarly twitted, and indeed the entire spirit of the Billy Hill phenomenon, as Babagenoush ably puts it, was to "air the profound mystification of the common man over the government's mystification of common sense."

Billy Hill became associated with migrants and HOBOES around 1936, and began to serve as a voice of the forgotten. His voice became more acerbic and less witty in this period, and even his name was distorted. Around 1937, Babagenoush says, Americans began to call all hoboes "Billy Hills," and by the following year this had become *hillbilly*. The association with country people—that is, those who looked like Billy Hill—soon followed.

Hobo

Hobo is an American slang term dating from the 1890s, when recession forced many workers onto the roads. It seems to have originated among former slaves, and to have passed into general working-class jargon by the 1910s. The slave connection suggests an African background, and evidence from folklore bears this out. In a series of folktales from the Gambia River basin—a major loading point for American slaves—Hooboo is the name of a legendary, wandering ghost. Some tales depict him as a former king who loses his influence and his possessions through sorcery. Others say he was a noted singer who challenged the wind demons to a yelling match and was reduced to tatters in the encounter. Whatever his crime, the tales agree that Hooboo dresses in threadbare, particolored clothing and that he must depend on strangers for his meals. In West Africa, then as now, it was considered wise to help the homeless in his name.

Holding the Bag

The masters of many trades and avocations send their apprentice members on wild goose chases as part of informal initiations. Thus a plumber's helper might be asked to fetch a left-handed monkey wrench, or a green machinist sent for elbow grease. Among campers and backpackers the favorite wild geese include the sky hook (for hanging pots over fires in treeless areas), the bucket of steam (to save boiling time), and the ubiquitous but uncapturable snipe. In a snipe hunt, the tenderfoot plays the honored role of *bag man*. It is his job to hold a canvas bag open in the middle of a snipe's "known" homing trail. The veteran campers, after giving him detailed instructions on how to hold the bag and how to attract the wary bird, disappear into the brush, supposedly to drive the quarry in his direction. The level of the newcomer's gullibility is then gauged by how long it takes him to figure out that no snipe ever ran into a sack, and that his plaintive cries of "Here, snipe, here, snipe" have been designed purely for the hilarity of his friends. Hence *holding the bag* in the sense of being cheated or made to look foolish. (When the phrase is used in the sense of "take responsibility for an illegal action," it of course refers to the captured bagman in a criminal gang, left holding the loot or other evidence after his accomplices have gotten away.)

Holy Smoke

Since the late Middle Ages, papal elections have been held in Vatican City's Sistine Chapel in a secret ballot process known as "scrutiny"—that is, close investigation of the candidates. For a new pope to be elected, two-thirds of the assembled cardinals, plus one, must agree. To keep the faithful outside the chapel apprised of its progress, if any, the conclave of cardinals burns its ballots after voting, sending smoke up the chimney as a sign. Black smoke, created by the addition of tar to the ballots, indicates that the two-thirds majority has not been reached; white smoke announces a new pope. Balloting may take days or even weeks, and in 1492, when the election of the Borgia pope Alexander VI was achieved after only one ballot, the event was widely viewed as nearly miraculous. The Roman expression *fumo santo*, or *holy smoke*, referring to the unusually early white plume, came to be used for anything unexpected or surprising.

Honeymoon

An often repeated folktale traces this term to Anglo-Saxon England, where newly married couples supposedly spent the first month, or "moon," of their lives together drinking honey or honey wine (mead) off in the forest. This is only partially true. Couples did spend a month of isolation after their weddings, but as the great Saxon scholar Brigitta Fitch-Wales shows in her study of marital customs *The Wed Bed*, what they did with the honey was not to drink it. Instead, they rubbed their bodies with the stuff and engaged in what Fitch-Wales calls "a primitive version of the Mazola party, where bride and groom would lovingly lick each other clean, for the duration of a full *honeymoon*." The practice, which was known as "honey dipping," gave us the endearment *honey*, for "sweetheart," and also the now archaic term *honey-tongued*, to describe a "sweet talker" or accomplished lover; when we speak of mellifluous (from the Latin for "honey flowing") speech, we are referring indirectly to the Saxon custom.

Hooch

Chinese laborers who were brought to California in the 1860s to work on the transcontinental railroad were relatively unfamiliar with strong drink, and when they first imbibed the nearly lethal liquids that passed for whiskey on the American frontier, they gave them an appropriate nickname: Hard liquor was *hua cha*, or "dragon tears." *Hoochah*, and then *hooch*, followed. The railroads sometimes paid their workers "bonuses" of whiskey in addition to—or in lieu of—wages, and as a result many ended up drunk and disorderly on the weekend. The worst offenders would be confined until they sobered up in what the Chinese called the *hua cha gow*, or "dragon tear cage." This quaint expression for the drunk tank gave us the term *hoosegow*, for jail.

Hoodwink

Medieval fairs, like modern carnivals, relied heavily for their income on midway games. One of the most popular of these games was the sleight-of-hand specialty called the Shell Game. In the Middle Ages, as today, a small object (often a pea) would be placed beneath one of three walnut shells, the shells would be rapidly shuffled on a table, and the customer would lay a wager on his ability to pick which shell held the pea. A good shell artist, of course, could remove the pea without the customer knowing it, so that whichever shell he picked, he lost the bet. But when the game was played fairly, the alert customer had a good chance of picking the right shell at least some of the time. Since penalties for cheating were severe (such as the loss of a hand), many shell games were quite honest, and this led, in thirteenth-century England, to a modification of the rules which gave us *hoodwink*.

What happened was that the London-based Mountebanks' Guild petitioned the Crown for assistance. They were losing so much income to sharp customers, they said, that gambling itself might be in jeopardy unless they could slightly "adjust" the odds. Their suggestion: Shell-game operators should work in twos, with one person working the table and the other standing just behind the customer. The second person, they said, should be permitted, at an unspecified point in the shuffling, to pull the customer's hood over his eyes, just for a second, so the chances of his guessing right would be reduced. The Crown, strapped by Crusade expenses and fearing the loss of guild taxes, agreed to the remarkable suggestion, and the practice, contemptuously known as *hood blinking* or *hood winking*, was instantly adopted throughout the realm. The contemporary expression *to pull the wool over someone's eyes* is also a reflection of the practice.

Although these phrases survive today, the practice itself was short-lived. In 1215, as is commonly known, the English King John signed the Magna Carta, granting rudimentary democratic rights to his barons. What is not so commonly known is that a month after the Great Charter was made law, he was also forced to sign a Parva Carta, or Lesser Charter, which outlawed not only *hoodwinking*, but also such older revenue-raising schemes as the *jus secondae noctis* and the "forward" tax on planned social improvements. (For more on these gimmicks, see EVEN STEVEN.)

Hooey

Hooey, which today means simply "nonsense," once meant a very particular kind of nonsense: the exaggerated, unprovable claims or promises of a demagogic politician. Throughout the 1930s the term was applied to the campaign statements of FDR and to the planks of his New Deal platform. But the original attribution was to Roosevelt's political rival, Huey Long, the Louisiana country lawyer who founded that state's political dynasty by appealing to the frustrations of the poor. Long, who served as governor from 1928 to 1931, then as U.S. senator until his assassination in 1935, used a magnetic personality and the spoils system to systematically transform Louisiana life. Corporate and other vested interests might have merely looked askance at the "Kingfish" when he introduced such reforms as the supplying of free textbooks for schoolchildren and the abolition of the poll tax; but when he advocated a dramatically progressive income tax and a guaranteed annual income in his famous Share the Wealth program, they denounced him as a spinner of fables, and *hooey* came to stand for any idea that had not (and, more importantly, should not) be tried.

From the Horse's Mouth

This is a modern, sanitized version of the nineteenth-century British army expression "from the whore's mouth." During the Napoleonic Wars, the British frequently employed prostitutes as spies. The information the women brought back from their French lovers was thought to be particularly reliable because of the ancient folk belief, common throughout northern Europe, that wine and sex bring out the truth: as the Latin adage has it, *in vino venereque veritas.* The Victorian transformation from *whore* to *horse*, while misleading, was perfectly understandable, for the two words had been confused since King Arthur's time, and the confusion was often "certified" by vulgar puns. Think, for example, of the dual meanings in English for such words as *ride*, *mount*, and *stallion*—or of the licentious sense of being *in the saddle.*

Beyond the mere linguistic confusion, the identification of horses with sexuality is an ancient one in the Indo-European tradition. Jaan Puhvel of the University of California, in his *Myth and Law Among the Indo-Europeans*, records numerous instances of horse-worship involving bestiality and general sexual license. Equinologist James Viscera, in private correspondence, has told me that the whore–horse connection goes back to the "Italian Stallion" ceremonies of Etruscan Italy, in which temple prostitutes stood in for divine horses during fertility rites.

Hot Seat

Probably the two best-known torture devices invented by medieval inquisitors were the rack and the iron maiden. The former survives today in the expression *racked with pain*, and the latter has lent its name to a musical group which takes pride in torturing the ears. A third, less publicized torture device was the French Inquisition's *chaise chaude*, the literal original of *hot seat*. This was a small metal chair which would be placed over a fire and to which the naked victim would be chained until he confessed to the inquisitor's fantasies. Giving someone this kind of *hot seat* frequently led to his death, and even in those rare cases when the victim survived the ordeal, his flesh bore the burn scars for life. Such unfortunates were known as *grillées*, or "the grilled ones," and when modern police interrogators speak of *grilling* a suspect, they are referring figuratively to what once was a very real practice.

Humble Pie

Richard Humble was the Ray Kroc of his day. In the middle of the eighteenth century, he started a chain of London eating establishments that were really little more than braziers in a doorway, and that specialized in extremely inexpensive "workmen's fare," especially fish and chips and shepherd's pies. To laborers who wanted a brief respite from a twelve- or thirteen-hour day, Humble's pie was a godsend: At tuppence a throw, there was nowhere in London you could beat the price. Precisely because his stands served such reasonably priced food, established restaurateurs viewed them with alarm and attempted to discredit them with lunchers. It was because of a whispering campaign mounted by these merchants in 1754 that *humble pie* came to have the connotation of cheapness in its negative sense, and that the idea of eating *humble pie* became associated with a loss of status.

Humble might have survived nonetheless had it not been for the next trick in the envious restaurateurs' bag. During the summer of 1755, the "news" was put around London that Humble's pies contained cat meat as well as beef. In the north of England this would have made no difference (see SKIN A CAT). In the south it was a telling blow, and Humble closed all his stands within a year. The leader of the London whispering cabal, incidentally, was a Chelsea pub owner named Hollington Poole; it is from his name that we get *dirty pool.*

Ignorance Is Bliss

The basic sense of this proverbial observation—that peace of mind may derive from an ignorance of the facts—is as old as the Roman poet Horace, who in his famous first Ode, *"Tu ne quaesieris,"* quipped that the best approach to questions about life and fate was "Don't ask." But the specific wording of the adage *Ignorance is bliss* comes from an anonymous Puritan allegory, the 1701 *Life of Folly,* which ridiculed Massachusetts public figures as representatives of competing orthodoxies. Cotton Mather, for example, because of his championing of science, appeared as microscope-toting Little Knowledge. His uncle, Decrease "Blue" Mather (see BLUE LAWS) was the obvious prototype for Dr. Daydream. Roger Williams, who had been exiled to Rhode Island for his allegiance to "inner light" and to the Indians, appeared as a feathered savage called Speak-in-Tongues. And an eccentric preacher named Samuel Bliss was represented by the character Ignorance. Hence the attributory tag "Ignorance is Bliss," which was much heard in Boston at the time.

Bliss had started out in the 1680s as an erudite minister, but the abuse of Scripture during the witch trials disillusioned him profoundly, and in 1698 he abjured "book learning" entirely, calling it, in a famous sermon, "a subtill snare of the vigilant demonn horde." Not only did he refuse to teach Scripture to the young—thus renouncing a major pastoral duty—but he shunned any contact, even aural, with the writings of other Puritan fathers, and thus became, like Williams, a de facto defender of "private devotion." Banished like Williams from the colony, he returned to Europe after 1700, where he became a painter of religious tableau. This occupation led him to popularize the English adage—so often erroneously ascribed to the Chinese—"One triptych is worth a thousand words."

Shortly after its appearance, the Mather family attempted to have all copies of *Life of Folly* burned, but one at least escaped the flames, and is preserved in the Harvard Library archives. The allegory's author has never been identified.

Indian Giver

An *Indian giver* is a person who presents a gift only to request it back—in other words, a lender in disguise. In spite of the term's implication, it was not the American Indians who initiated this practice; indeed, as in most traditional societies where exchange is defined as reciprocity, the taking back of a gift among the Indians would have been simply unthinkable. Not so, of course, among the whites, who considered it entirely acceptable to offer a treaty in January and disavow it in June. The original *Indian givers*, then, were those who gave things *to* the Indians—blankets, reservations, their word—and then retracted them at a later date. The vernacular has conveniently obscured this point by hinting that the recipients were the givers.

Makes Jack a Dull Boy

The adage "All work and no play *makes Jack a dull boy*" has an obvious, common-sense logic, but there is also a hidden meaning to the expression. Since the 1830s the American pocket knife

has been popularly known as a jack knife, from the English term
jack for "man" or "boy." In the same decade, nonfolding hunting
knives came to be known as bowie knives, from their erroneous
association with Jim Bowie. Pocket knives had to be kept sharp,
since they were used in close work such as wood carving and
HAIRSPLITTING. This was not as true for the bowie. Its weight made
it valuable as a weapon even when it had lost its edge, and there
is an Ozark tradition that says the famous bear which Davy Crock-
ett killed with his bowie knife was not stabbed, but brained to
death with the blade. It is this contrast between the two types of
knives to which the adage alludes. A person who used his pocket
knife in an edge-damaging enterprise such as whittling would
have to sharpen it frequently, and this was done by "playing" it
on a whetstone. If he neglected to give it the right amount of
"play," it would soon be as dull as a bowie—in Tennessee dialect, *one dull boy.*

In a Jam

The original phrase was "in *the* jam," and it arose among Appalachian woodsmen around 1800 in reference to a briefly popular hunting technique. Capitalizing on the fondness of raccoons and skunks for nocturnal pilferage, hunters would place earthenware pots of fruit preserves near their campfires and wait in the shadows with loaded shotguns. When a scavenger, smelling the bait, climbed into the pot to investigate, the hunters would whisper to each other that the quarry was "in the jam," and promptly blow it to hell—pot and all. The practice rapidly died out as the shooters discovered that the combination of potsherds and jam made a particularly foul-tasting stew.

The use of *jam* to describe any difficult situation spread up and down the Eastern Seaboard in the decade before the War of 1812. By the final year of that conflict the usage had spawned an antonym: In a pamphlet published in New Orleans in February 1815, we find the pirate Jean Lafitte, who had passed British battle plans on to Andrew Jackson, being applauded for "helping our worthy Old Hickory out of a mighty sticky bit of jam"—a courtesy never extended to raccoons.

Jeepers

The single word *jeepers* was the punch line of one of the most popular shaggy-dog stories of World War II. The tale involved— in addition to the inevitable shaggy dog—a brace of army mules, a regiment of German soldiers dressed in lederhosen, General Eisenhower's barber, several planeloads of uncooked chipped beef, and a quartet of WACs (see WACKY) who showed up mysteriously in one army post after another, driving a purple jeep; it was they who were known as the *jeepers*. Enormously popular on the western front, the story gave rise to the curt comment *jeepers* first as a code word for incredulity (meaning "I can't believe you're boring me with this drivel"), then as an exclamation of mock surprise, and finally as a term of genuine surprise. Even in its many abbreviated versions, the story is too long to repeat here. For those interested in the details, a semi-official "text" (approved by the International Aural History Society) is given in British field commander General Twice Exalted B. S. Montgomery-McArthur's memoir of the 1944 campaigns, *How I Won the War.*

Jerry-Built

We say that something inexpertly constructed is *jerry-built* not because *jerry* sounds like *jury* (as in "jury rigged"), or because the Germans ("Jerries" in World War I) were supposed to be lousy carpenters, or because there was, in Partridge's citation, "a rascally speculating builder" in nineteenth-century Liverpool who consistently built houses that fell apart. Here's the real reason. A *jerry,* from about 1850, was what Partridge himself calls "a low beer house." It got its name from the vintner's term jeroboam for a huge bottle, which in turn was named after the Biblical King Jeroboam, spoken of as a "mighty man of valor." Builders who spent time in such beer houses were said to be "jerried," and a jerried builder was of course not up to par. Fetch and Tarry cite numerous letters to London newspapers in the 1860s from homeowners whose contractors had "jerried them off" by doing work after returning from the jerry. A street song of the era mocked a "happy jerry builder" named Paddy Ryan who was a victim of his own excess in this regard:

> *Paddy took a hammer after twenty pints of brew,*
> *Set a nail upon the floor and drove it through his shoe.*

This song, incidentally, gave us *drunk driver* to describe anyone doing work while under the influence.

Jim Dandy

A *jim dandy* is someone or something exceptional, and the original Jim Dandy was certainly that. At a time when horse racing in the West was still largely the sport of kings, British monarch James I owned a stable that was the envy of Europe. At Epsom Downs, the British track that he helped to establish, he successfully took on comers from many nations, and distinguished himself particularly against France's Cardinal Richelieu, whose personal mount, D'Artagnan, posed constant but vain threats to English primacy. One reason for the Stuart king's unbroken string was the brilliant Arabian stallion Jim's Dandy. *Dandy* is a Scottish nickname for Andrew, and the horse was a gift of Scottish admirers. So unbeatable was it at Epsom Downs that Richelieu claimed that if Louis XIII would permit it, he would gladly give back Normandy for the stallion; this facetious comment became the basis for the anti-Gallic jibe, "A horse, a horse, my kingdom for a horse." Because of the stallion's racing prowess, the Jacobean phrase "a Jim's Dandy" meant anything invincible or extraordinary.

Jimmy

Jimmy O'Doyle was an Irish immigrant to New York City hired by the police department in the 1890s chiefly because of his size. O'Doyle weighed over 400 pounds. The boys in blue used him as a battering ram to break down the locked doors of crime suspects. To *jimmy* a lock in those days thus meant to break through it by force majeure; only later did the expression come to be applied to other irregular methods of gaining entry, such as picking the lock with bobby pins or special tools.

O'Doyle was a minor celebrity toward the end of the century. In addition to working for the police, he was a frequent attraction on the carnival circuit and, during the 1897 Christmas season, was the city's official Santa Claus. It is a little known fact of social history that little Virginia O'Hanlon, whose query to the New York *Sun* prompted the classic reply, "Yes, Virginia, there is a Santa Claus," expressed doubt not about flying reindeer or the North Pole, but about how O'Doyle could get down a chimney.

Walter Marcy, in his charming book *Gaslight Gotham*, calls O'Doyle "a jovial, rather slow-witted soul" whose principal amusement, aside from *jimmying* doors, was downing gallons of beer at a time. His penchant for the hops did not endear him to the city's temperance movement, which condemned him as a poor example to children and eventually turned popular sentiment against him. The police department let him go in 1902. A year later he returned to his native land where, as Marcy notes coyly, "the opponents of John Barleycorn had barely gotten a foot in the door."

John

Numerous eponymologists have contended that the John behind this term for "bathroom" was an English nobleman, Sir John Herrington, who invented a flush toilet during Henry VIII's reign. This is fakelore of a particularly tendentious and chauvinistic variety. As is demonstrated clearly in the Académie Française Scatologique's recent study, the actual inventor of this device was one Jean Privet, a soldier who had fought in Francis I's wars against Henry and who, when news of "Herrington's" invention broke, was a prisoner of the English outside of London. The Académie study gives solid evidence, including a royal pardon issued to Privet, that the Frenchman bargained for his release with the toilet's designs, and that Herrington was a mere legal fiction meant to obscure the soldier's contribution to English hygiene. The brazenness of Henry's lawyers knew no bounds. Not only did they issue broadsides announcing the inventor's name as John (an obvious sleight-of-mouth on the original *Jean*) but they even translated his designation *cabinet de l'eau* into the instantly popular Anglicism "water closet," and—as a final indignity—appropriated his family name for English *privy.*

To correct this four-centuries-old miscarriage of justice, the Académie in 1985 issued a formal complaint to the British government, asking that Privet's name be restored to its rightful place of honor and that reparations in the amount of ten pounds be paid to the Académie on behalf of Privet's descendants. The more whimsical members of Parliament were debating the proposition in 1986 when Mr. Crippen, Liberal of Berks, discovered a clause which stipulated that the ten pounds should be treated as sixteenth-century money invested at that time and compounded annually. Since the resulting reparations to the Académie would have amounted to three times the British national debt, the idea was hastily abandoned, with Crippen expressing the consensus of the House: "This time those froggies have gone too far."

John Doe/Jane Doe

The legal fictions *John Doe* and *Jane Doe* were at first criminals', not attorneys', inventions. Originating in the vice-ridden back streets of eighteenth-century London, they served much the same purpose there as *Smith* and *Jones* do today: They were the conventional pseudonyms offered police by suspicious characters brought in for questioning. Magistrates heard these false names so often that by the end of the century they adopted them defensively as their own, so that they became legal shorthand for *person.*

Long Johns

Friedrich Ludwig Jahn, a German educator, founded modern gymnastics in 1811 as a way of marshaling his nation's physical and mental prowess against what he saw as Napoleonic tyranny. The popularity of his movement waxed and waned, and his achievement was not fully recognized until 1840, when he received the coveted Iron Cross. Among the specific contributions he made to the development of the sport were the invention of the horizontal and parallel bars, the side horse, and the balance beam. Jahn also introduced a tight-fitting, full-body exercise costume that foreshadowed the leotard by fifty years. It was called the *lang Jahn*, or "long Jahn," in his honor. In America, where such costumes were in demand as undergarments among Western settlers and miners, they became known as *long johns*.

Keeping Up with the Joneses

The daredevil team of Winston and Myra Jones were the Flying Wallendas of the 1920s. At a time when flagpole sitting, wing walking, and barreling over Niagara Falls were becoming increasingly popular, the Joneses set the pace for other loonies by the extravagance of their hazardous feats. Originally an aerial duo, they left the Texas-based Big Bend Rodeo and Circus Company in 1924 to seek greener pastures on their own. They found them first in the Midwest, where they specialized in "Ogallala surfing" (surfing on the vast underground Ogallala Aquifer) and, after 1926, in the East and in Europe, where their publicly announced willingness to take up any challenge for money (their motto was "Your dough, we go") led to a string of unique performances. In 1927 they climbed the Eiffel Tower, then the tallest structure in the world. In 1928, in New York, they swam first the East River, then the Hudson, and finally the treacherous Passaic Narrows, thus completing the so-called Triple Crown of swimming in the space of one day. In the year of the stock market crash, when so many ruined investors were jumping from buildings, they advertised themselves as "defenestration experts" and made an estimated one million dollars catching would-be suicides before they landed.

By the end of the decade the Joneses were so famous that Robert Ripley had featured them sixteen times, and Chicago cartoonist B. V. Doren had started a weekly panel devoted entirely to their exploits. It was not conspicuous consumption, but rather this newspaper feature, entitled "Keeping Up with the Joneses," that gave us the popular expression. The feature, and the Joneses themselves, expired in 1931, when they ended their careers in a freakish accident. In December 1930, as a promotional stunt, the New York Public Library had hired them to read its entire circus collection while perched on the library roof. They managed this feat without trouble, finishing the last book in July, but by that time they had inhaled so much library dust that they died of a mutual case of "BOOKWORM lung."

Sober as a Judge

The source of this phrase was ancient Greece, where it was oddly ambivalent. Throughout much of the Athenian experiment with democracy, a characteristic respect for rational discourse (*logos*) warred with an older and, some would say, more characteristic Greek attraction to the irrational—and this latter attraction was by no means publicly disavowed. In fact, the principal quality of a good public servant—whether he was a legislator, an archon, or a judge—was thought to be a sense of cosmic "balance" between what Nietzsche later called "Apollonian" sobriety and "Dionysian" excess. A judge needed to be able to reason clearly, to be sure. But to the Greeks "reasoning clearly" did not mean the same thing as being sober. It meant, in effect, being clear-eyed and intoxicated at the same time—being so fired with the spirit of the law that you could dispense at will with the letter. Thus the best judges, according to Greek tradition, were expert not in *logos* but in *methos*. This archaic term meant both "method" and "wine." When a Greek praised a lawmaker for being "methodical," he meant the person was alogically inspired, and to be as sober as a judge (*methos dikastou*) was to be "drunk" with a wisdom beyond logic.

Kangaroo Court

The Australian answer to William Lynch, whose *vigilante* tactics gave us lynch law, was a sheepherder turned "judge" named Jeremy Wanker. He lived at the end of the last century, when Australia was still wilder than the Old West, and when sheep-rustling was as common in the outback as cattle-thieving had been on the plains. Wanker led a Queensland "citizens' correction" organization that was notorious for its summary hangings. In the most celebrated episode of its bloody history, the group captured a trio of vagabonds who happened to be near Wanker's ranch on the day after two sheep disappeared. Outback historian Chloe Schooner describes the incident in her biography of Wanker, *The Kangaroo King*: "The three wanderers, protesting that they deserved a proper hearing, were treated to the epitome of Wanker's justice. Agreeing they should be tried by their peers, he sent his hands into the bush to fetch a brace of kangaroos. He tethered the animals in two neat rows, like the jurors at a colonial hearing, and ordered the vagabonds to make their defense. Wanker then 'interpreted' the findings of the marsupials, and ordered the trio strung up. From this travesty we get *kangaroo court*."

Kick the Bucket

It has often been stated, erroneously, that this euphemism for dying refers to hanging. The theory is that, in the days before the widespread use of scaffolds, the condemned man would be stood on a bucket, the rope would be put around his neck, and the bucket would be kicked out from under him; or, in an even more distasteful variation, he would be left standing on the bucket until he himself kicked it out. The absurdity of this explanation becomes evident when you recall that scaffolds were invented *before* buckets, by a good three and a half years.

The actual origin of the expression is found in Andrée Chappuis's charming 1869 memoir, *Tales of Old New Awlins*. As Mlle. Chappuis tells it, in the 1820s there was a notorious brawler called Claude Bouchet who worked as a gambling-house bouncer and who was universally known in the Latin Quarter as the "Medusa of Bourbon Street." The nickname referred to the fact that "he was thought to be as ugly as the Gorgon, and in addition was deadly to cross. When Bouchet was in one of his snits—which was often—brave men would avoid him like the plague, for he had turned many to stone with his fists."

One of the ill-tempered bouncer's victims, Chappuis says, was a dandified gambler from upriver who had not heard of the Gorgon's reputation: "One summer evening the two men passed in the street. The Gorgon shoved the gambler from his path and kept walking, but the newcomer wouldn't let it go. He picked himself up, ran after Bouchet, and planted a boot in the seat of his pants. Of course he was dead in five minutes, and ever after that, to "kick the Bouchet" was a Bourbon Street expression for dying. It was some Yankee tourist, I believe, who carried the term back up North, mispronouncing it in the process so it came out *kick the bucket*."

Treat Someone With Kid Gloves

The fingerless "gloves" that are now worn by golf pros and racing car drivers are the modern version of a style first worn by the wealthy in fourteenth-century England. Because their peculiar design made them relatively useless as protection in hard labor, they were not adopted, as so many other fashions were, by the country's working classes; in fact workers referred to them contemptuously as "false" gloves or "kidding" gloves. The expression *treat someone with kid gloves* was a further swipe at ruling-class privilege: It mocked the aristocracy's supposed delicacy by imputing gentleness to the wearers of such apparel—at precisely the point in English history when "gentility" and peasant oppression went together. In the words of the rebel monk Alec of Yarrow, who narrowly escaped execution for his part in the 1381 Peasants' Rising:

> *Theye worke werste erthe in Goddes love*
> *To stay the starke handes of kiddes glove.*

The "worst earth" referred to here is the marginally productive land to which many a lord would consign his serfs and tenant holders—a legally sanctioned abuse which did nothing to endear the peasants to the wearers of "kidding" gloves.

Whole Kit and Caboodle

A World War I expression, this referred collectively to the contents of a soldier's kit bag, or knapsack, and of his pockets, where he kept his money, or "boodle." The *ca* prefix in *caboodle* is a contraction of *camp*, and the caboodle of the camp-based infantryman would cover such incidental commissary items as magazines, candy, and cigarettes. In the trenches one's *whole kit and caboodle* came to be a shorthand for "everything"—that is, the entire "estate" of the man in the field—and the expression "go out *kit and caboodle*" meant to be killed carrying everything you owned.

The kit bag was named for Herbert Kitchener, the general who spearheaded the British conquest of the Sudan in the 1890s and who was secretary of state for war during World War I. *Boodle*, an eighteenth-century highwayman's term, is a fanciful corruption of *booty*.

On the Lam

Before Harry Houdini, there was Willie "the Turnkey" Lamm (1780?–1815), a minor burglar and pettifogger who gained a reputation in his day for multiple prison escapes. First imprisoned in 1813 for pickpocketing, Willie cheated the judge by disappearing the night before his trial, and in the following three years repeated the trick on five other judges, even managing in 1814 to extricate himself from notorious Dartmoor Prison, the English equivalent of Devil's Island.

Lamm's dexterity with penknives and hairpins so enchanted the London poor that they made him a popular hero, and his name, truncated to *lam*, became an equivalent for escape or freedom. But Willie himself fell "off the lam" when he was arrested in 1815 for engineering the notorious Leicester Bath House Robbery. Although he had not actually been present, he was shown to have been the brains behind the plan that left six peers of the realm with their pockets empty and their pants literally down. Found guilty of "perverse corporation"—British legalese for "bad company"—he was hanged on July 19, and evidently went out with no regrets. His last comment, according to Brimmer's *Noted Rogues*, was, "I look forward to picking the lock of the Pearly Gates."

Lame Duck

Today a *lame duck* is a politician who has failed in a bid for reelection and who must sit out his term as if "crippled," that is, with nothing to look forward to. In the eighteenth century the expression was applied to others in a crippled position: stockbrokers who could not meet their debts. Before that, a *lame duck* was a prostitute. British hookers had been known as *doxies* since the middle of the sixteenth century, when many of them plied their trade along the docks. A *doxy*, or "duck," became "lame" when, through ill health or simply age, she had lost the looks that had once earned her keep. At that point, like today's politicians, she would still be in business but going nowhere.

Have a Lark

Lark in the sense of "good times" or "merriment" is the Anglicized truncation of the more specific French phrase *l'arc de joie*, which means literally "the arch of joy." Arches of joy were the elaborate, half-moon-shaped jeweled headdresses that were so popular among Mardi Gras marchers in eighteenth- and nineteenth-century New Orleans. Massive architectural constructions, they could measure up to five feet in diameter and were responsible for many neck injuries each season. As a result of these injuries, which reflected badly on the city's carefree image, the New Orleans city council banned the headpieces in 1898, and mounted a vigorous public health campaign denouncing them as *l'arcs de fou*, or "arches of the fool." Various illegal "Lark Clubs" sustained the tradition for a while, and even held clandestine "Mardi Mince" marches at which they ridiculed the governmental strictures. But by 1900, partly as a result of the health campaign and partly because of the rising expense of constructing the *arcs*, they had been largely replaced in public favor by the more sedate feather-and-bangle headdresses of today.

Laugh Up One's Sleeve

To *laugh up one's sleeve* at a person is to make fun of him surreptitiously. The expression is what Sabine Baring-Gould would have called a "strange survival," for the original meaning was anything but surreptitious. In sixteenth-century Italy, it was a widespread folk belief that the size and thickness of a man's forearm reflected the size and thickness of his sexual organ; the French at the time had a similar belief connecting the penis and the nose. Peering into a person's sleeve and laughing at what you saw there, then, was a pointed sexual insult, and one that usually led to a duel. The great Renaissance "insult teacher" Girolamo Vitelloni (see VITTLES) put this practice into the give-and-take category of "insult gestures," or *gestos offensivos*. His advice was that the ostentatious sleeve peering be used directly after complimenting a person on his amatory prowess.

It was also Vitelloni who transformed the physical form of this traditional gesture, so that the insulter laughed up his *own* sleeve rather than up or into his opponent's. The logic for the change was clear enough. In the words of William Foxpaw's 1537 translation of Vitelloni's manual, "That ye may not lose a nose by the too close mockerie of the person's member, it bee hartily advized that ye laugh unto youre owne sleeve, so that hee take up your meening at a safe distance."

Lead Balloon

To go over like a *lead balloon* is to be a dismal failure, a BOMB. The obvious derivation is not the actual one. A *ballon* in France is both a balloon and a large-capacity, balloon-shaped wine glass. Typically these are made of glass, so that the drinker may savor the appearance as well as the taste of the wine. *Ballon*-style goblets made of lead (*plomb*) were introduced by a Marseilles manufacturer during the notorious glass shortage of the 1870s. This was well before toxicologists had come to understand the dangers of lead poisoning, and so there were no medical objections to the innovation. Fortunately, there were aesthetic ones: The French simply could not abide the notion of quaffing their "fermented sunlight" from opaque containers. The *lead balloon* idea never got off the ground, except to give the language one more synonym for failure: *ballon du plomb*.

Turn Over a New Leaf

Although most commentators say that *leaf* in this expression means the flyleaf, or any page, of a book, that is not the phrase's origin. The reference is not to books but to trees. In ancient times throughout the British Isles, it was considered lucky to be the first to "catch the spring," that is, to spot the appearance of new foliage, and particularly fortunate to see the first leaf, rather than bud, on an oak tree. New leaves were also plucked from oaks, to be used in a soothsaying ceremony. In this ceremony the high priest would be presented with all the new leaves that had been collected in the thirteen days prior to the vernal equinox, and he would read the village's fortune in the leaves' veins. Since the reading involved meticulous inspection and much turning over of the leaves, the Old English phrase *leef tyrnan* came to be a shorthand first for the ceremony, then for the spring new year activities in general, and finally for the very idea of newness.

Leap Year

When Julius Caesar set out to revise the Roman calendar, he encountered the same problem that had plagued other early calendar makers: how to overcome the inconvenient fact that the earth took 365¼, not a clean 365, days to make its revolution around the sun. He solved this celestial dilemma by introducing the now well-known gimmick of the *leap year*—the addition of an extra day every four years to make up for the four "lost" quarters. Calendar experts explain the term *leap year* by saying that, in a 365-day system, a date that is a Monday in one year becomes a Tuesday in the second, a Wednesday in the third, and a Thursday in the fourth, which would lead to infinite regression unless in the fourth year Thursday was "leaped over" for Friday.

If that sounds as confusing to you as it does to me, you can imagine how it sounded to a Roman soldier who worked in numbers like CCCLXV, and who had never heard of fractions or New Math. In fact it was precisely Caesar's confusion, and not the leaped-over Thursday, that gave us the term in the first place. The emperor had hired the astronomer Sosigenes to help him with his calculations. When, after much deliberation, they finally thought of adding up the lost quarters, they did exactly what we would have done: They leaped in the air for joy. Sallust reports that this occurred in the Forum in 45 B.C., and that with Caesar's personal urging the idea of making February 29 an official "leaping day" soon became a bill in the senate. Caesar's idea was that on this *dies saltus* all Romans would hop to work in his calendar's honor. He was killed, of course, before the bill could be passed. Erika Seagull believes that the bill itself, and not Caesar's supposed "kingly" ambitions, was the real reason for his assassination.

Break a Leg

Break a leg is the traditional good-luck wish given to an actor about to go on. The apparent absurdity of the expression is explained by the fact that *leg* (pronounced "ledge") is an old shortened form for *legend*. To "break a legend" meant to outshine the work of a former, legendary performer. For this reason *Break a leg* was a particularly common greeting to an actor about to try a role which had recently been made famous by another. It was also very widely heard during the heated theatrical rivalries of the last century, when the fans of a given STAR performer would use it as a taunt against their rivals.

Pulling One's Leg

Three years after Captain James Cook met his death at the hands of Hawaiian natives, his first mate Alastair Slyke was given command of the frigate *Enterprise* and told by the British admiralty to seek out and punish Cook's murderers. Slyke was a feisty Yorkshireman who knew more of brawling than of navigation, and his 1781–1782 voyage produced neither culprits nor revenge. What it did bring back to England was the expression *pulling one's leg.*

According to Slyke's *Journal*, in October 1781 the *Enterprise* put in at an island approximately 200 miles south of Tahiti. Natives beckoned from the shore, "laughing and brandishing palm fronds." "Cheered by the sight of their levity," Slyke reported, "we lowered a boat and pulled in. Aside from myself, there was in the boat Mr. Higgins, our first mate Mr. Hickock, and six tars. The friendly appearance of the natives had caused us to disembark unarmed, and this proved at once to be imprudent. Upon landing we were roughly seized by the savages, who spread-eagled us all on the sand and performed upon our prostrate bodies a ceremony I must blush to relate.

"With two natives each at our arms, two others fastened on our legs, and began slowly and with malicious glee to pull them wide, much as a child pulls a wishbone. We all expected to be torn apart, and committed our souls to the Almighty. Yet at the initial sign of our distress, the queer ordeal instantly ended. It was Mr. Higgins, I believe, who cried out. Hearing his cry, our tormentors released our limbs and let us up, all the while laughing uncontrollably and muttering, over and over, what sounded to my ears like 'Tutu kiki.' Believing the wretches to be insane, and being unimpeded in our progress toward the boat, we returned in some haste to the ship and departed with their derision in our ears.

"Two days later we were told by the less whimsical inhabitants of a neighboring island that our leg-pulling hosts had been *Tutu kikini*, or 'jesters for the great lord Tutu.' The expression we had heard meant 'Tutu laughs.' Evidently they had never intended us harm, but were only following the precepts of their religion, which demanded such mock sacrifice of travelers because, as we were solemly informed, *Tutu malu kiki uguliki*, that is, 'Tutu must eat laughter or he dies.' I bring this custom to the public's attention that we may be mindful of the fortunate accident of Christian birth."

Slyke's *Journal* was published in 1783, enjoyed a brief vogue among booksellers, and spread *pulling one's leg* throughout England. The author lived to see its success, but died late in 1784, the victim of a dormant case of breadfruit poisoning.

Hand Someone a Line

In today's idiom, the "line" referred to here is the plausible argument of a liar, such as a stereotypical used-car dealer or a seducer. Originally, the line was an actual cord: a length of rope which a jokester would entrust to the victim of a practical joke. In Guy Smiley's recent catalog of traditional "insult games,"

Hoaxes, Jokeses, and Eye Pokeses, we find that the so-called Birmingham Rope Trick was extremely popular in eighteenth-century England. This is the way he describes it:

"The prankster would be dressed as a surveyor and would carry a length of coiled rope. Accosting his victim on a city street, he would claim to be doing an official building survey or something of the kind, and to have been caught shorthanded. 'Would you be so kind, Sir, as to hold on to one end of this rope while I connect the other to my apparatus around the corner?' Should the gullible passer-by agree, the trickster would then retreat around the corner, playing out the rope very gravely, until he happened upon another likely prospect—to whom he would present the *other* end! Then, with both marks in tow, he would disappear into the crowd, chuckling that he had handed them both a line."

The use of *mark* is interesting here. Smiley points out that it originated in this same Birmingham amusement. To make their proposition seem more believable, rope tricksters would often knot their props at regular intervals, so that they looked like measuring or "marking" lines. The victims would be asked to serve as "markers" or simply marks, and soon the word came to stand for the person taken in by any practical joke or professional swindle. (See also HOLDING THE BAG.)

Crazy as a Loon

This is a New England expression, referring to the courtship display of the common loon, *Gavia immer*. To attract a mate, the male bird rises up on its rather stubby legs and performs a tremulous, unsteady "dance" which reminded early settlers of epileptic spasms. In an age when epilepsy was frequently mistaken for insanity, the link between the bird's twitching and "mad" behavior was inevitable.

Of course, many other birds enact similar "crazy" displays, and for a time New Englanders also spoke of eccentrics as "grouse hoppers" and as being "nutty as a cormorant." Why did the loon connection in particular prove so durable? Probably because of the traditional association of odd behavior with the moon, which in Latin is *luna.* The bird's name sounded, quite coincidentally, like a shortened form of *lunatic.*

Knocked for a Loop

Loopy is old English slang for "eccentric" or "crazy." Some authorities believe the reference is to the circular, repetitious speech of some mentally unbalanced persons. Others see it as a comment on their walking in circles. Whichever interpretation is correct, it's clear that the phrases *knocked into a loop* and *knocked for a loop* were street slang, by about 1730, for anyone not completely in control of his faculties. It was applied specifically to punchdrunk pugilists in the era of bare-knuckle boxing and gradually extended in this century to anyone who had been sorely beaten in an engagement, whether physical, social, or financial.

The chief defender of the idea that *loopy* first referred to circular speech is the British psycholinguist Z. Z. Quinine. His theory that all human speech may be viewed as essentially repetitious has found great favor among computer enthusiasts, who have incorporated his definition of *loop* into program designs. The major champion of the circle-walking theory, now deceased, was the French scholar J.-J. Mallou (see OFF YOUR ROCKER), who traced numerous attempts on the part of nineteenth-century psychologists to undo the circularity of schizophrenic behavior by forcing patients to walk in straight lines. This "form follows function" retraining technique led to no recorded cures, but of course it did influence scientific thinking; Mallou is quite right in seeing it as "proto-behaviorism at its most bizarre."

Loophole

Before this term began to be applied to the law about a hundred years ago, it was used mainly by sheepherders. In the sheep-raising region of southern France, herders would join forces once or twice a year to rid the area of wolves. One of the most popular methods of dispatching them was the communitywide "enclosure hunt." The herders would encircle a large area known to contain the troublesome predators and gradually tighten the circle while beating bushes to drive the wolves toward the center. If the hunt went as planned, the animals then could be easily shot. But cagy wolves often slipped the trap by finding holes in the tightening human perimeter, and these spaces between the hunters became known, reasonably enough, as *troux du loup*, or "wolf holes." Transported to England around 1850, the expression was only partially translated, so that English herders, adopting the practice, spoke of "holes of loup" and ultimately "loupholes."

The application of the term to the law was accomplished by about 1900, and this seems to have come about in a straightforward manner, by simple diffusion based on resemblance. There is no truth to the suggestion, made rather whimsically by Yarrowville, that *loup* was Cockney rhyming slang for lawyer. The formula he gives is "Hole of loup = toup," where *toup* is the barrister's wig, or toupee. This clever guess, as might be expected of Yarrowville, betrays a thorough misunderstanding of Cockney rhyme.

Holy Mackerel

This expression has nothing to do with the supposed false piety of Roman Catholics, contemptuously called "mackerel snappers" by Protestants. Actually, it is a very Catholic term, having arisen in medieval France a century before Martin Luther's birth. At that time the Feast of Fools was still celebrated, as a way of poking fun at both clerical and secular authority, and thus defusing popular resentment at privilege. During this annual celebration, a Boy Bishop and a Lord of Misrule would be elected, and the most beloved saints would be ridiculed. In the Parisian version of the holiday, townspeople would even make up their own saints to mock the very idea of canonization, and would parade them in effigy through the streets. Among the most popular of these ad hoc sham saints, always represented by a nattily dressed effigy, was the supposed patron of adulterers, Saint Maquereau. *Maquereau*, or "mackerel," is underworld argot for "pimp" or "panderer," and the expression *aussi croyable que Saint Maquereau*, or "as believable as Saint Mackerel," was a common intimation of incredulity. English students at the Sorbonne managed to broaden the meaning in bringing it home, so that "sainted mackerel," and later *holy mackerel*, became mere registers of surprise.

Mad as a Wet Hen

The Anglo-Saxon legislative council was known as the *Witangemot*, or assembly of the *witan*; *witan* was the plural of *wite*, a sage, counselor, or "wite-ness." To the Romans who conquered Britain in the first century A.D., the deliberations of this council—with its frenzied enthusiasm, its name-calling, and its brandishing of weapons—were as far removed from sedate Roman lawmaking as the barbaric island speech was from Latin. The Roman jibe *tam furiosus quam witan* was the progenitor of the English "mad (or angry) as the *witan*," eventually corrupted into its present form. Yarrowville's suggestion that the wet hen of the expression was the Great Hen of Wetmore—the "fowl heroine of a lost tenth-century fable"—is, like most of his suggestions, charming nonsense.

To reduce the turmoil of *witan* meetings, the Romans introduced a custom known as *transmissio cornus*, or "passing the horn." The idea was the same as that governing the Egyptian system of PASSING THE BUCK: One person would speak at a time, with his authority for doing so being his temporary possession of a deer horn (*cornu*); passing the horn to another would count as transmission of the right to speak. The system was immediately subverted by speakers bringing along their own horns and using them to emphasize points as they formerly had utilized their weapons. It is from this corrupted Roman innovation that we get *horn in*, for interrupt.

Madcap

A *madcap* today is a person, but in the Middle Ages it was an actual cap, worn by young people with impetuous or *madcap* qualities. They were the so-called scholar-fools of France and England—university students who had left school before taking a doctorate, usually after a disagreement with the authorities over dress codes or other regulations. Modeling their behavior on that of court jesters, they traveled from one college town to another, singing rude street songs, mocking the pretensions of the formally educated, and in some cases actually destabilizing university communities by "tutoring" students for free with false information.

The attitude of academicians to these dropouts ranged from amusement to outright hostility, but everyone agreed they were colorful. The typical scholar-fool costume, a parody of academic dress, was a brazenly patched or particolored gown, ermine-topped boots (these were expressly forbidden by most dress codes), and a head covering that gave them the name "mad cappers." Since most of them held master's degrees, they had the right to wear the tufted birettas that were the mark of graduate scholars. Instead of wearing them conventionally, they sewed baskets or flat trenchers on top of them, filled them with fruit, and walked about like so many Carmen Mirandas, declaring that they were scholars of "apple lore" or "peach studies." The fruit also doubled as their food and as stage props for what one Exeter cleric called "these popinjays' incessant jugglings."

It has been suggested by some historians that the modern mortarboard may be derived from the fruit-filled caps of the scholarfools. A more certain legacy includes the word *madcap*, and one other phrase relating to madness. Since these eccentrics were the first generation of college dropouts, they were, ipso facto, the first to *take leave of their faculties.* The double entendre existed even in the thirteenth century—much to the delight of their detractors.

Money to Burn

Anyone familiar with the period of the Weimar Republic has seen pictures of dazed Germans pushing wheelbarrows, filled to overflowing with worthless, inflated paper money. The implication of the pictures is that the notes were about to be exchanged for goods and services, but sometimes that is not what happened. As in any severely stretched economy, barter and black marketeering often took over, and the government's money was used for a novel, nonexchange purpose. By the mid-1920s many Germans found that their bank notes were worth more as fuel than they would have been worth in buying bread—or, for that matter, in buying wood. So the wheelbarrowsful of paper were simply burned. This practice gave rise to two expressions that we use in modified form. When we *throw another log on the fire*, we are recalling the Weimar quip *werfen noch einen Lüge*, or "to throw another (government) lie into the fireplace." And when we speak of having *money to burn* as an indication of great wealth, we are ironically recalling a time when "great wealth" had no purchasing power.

Monkey on One's Back

This colorful metaphor for drug addiction was a product of the Turkish underworld—specifically, of the Istanbul drug culture that flourished around the turn of the century. Heroin addiction in those days was usually supported not by thievery but by begging, and to take the fullest advantage of their street time, many addicts took to keeping monkeys. Not only could the beasts be trained to beg—thus maintaining their owner's "draw" while he was on the nod—but in extreme duress they could be visibly mutilated (blinded, dismembered, scarred) as a means of eliciting pity. To have a *monkey on your back*, therefore, meant that you were a slave to heroin; to "have a blinded monkey" was even worse: It meant you were so far gone you had put out your pet's eyes so it would attract greater sympathy from passersby.

Mud in Your Eye

When William the Conqueror defeated the English King Harold's Saxon army at the Battle of Hastings in 1066, he ushered in centuries of Norman rule that were continually bedeviled by Saxon resentment. That resentment is mirrored in the Robin Hood story cycles, in which Sherwood outlawry is a version of Saxon populism, waged valiantly against Norman tyranny; and it is mirrored less obviously in the expression *mud in your eye.*

In the Middle Ages, mud was a kind of medicine; healers used it to stanch bleeding wounds, and it was thought to be a remedy against snakebite. According to legend, Harold had died at Hastings pierced by an arrow through his eye; the original form of the toast "Here's *mud in your eye*" (so says the Venerable Bean) was "Here's mud in *his* eye." Part magic formula and part underground password, the expression was shorthand among Saxons for the hope that their dead king might yet return if they could put enough mud on his wound. After the Normans discovered the subversive intent of the phrase, uttering it in their presence could mean death, and so it was modified to its current form. To toast a person with the phrase *mud in your eye* meant you were wishing him good sight—something not even the Normans could proscribe.

Name Is Mud

Virtually all etymologists (including the skeptical Ronald and Peck) accept the often told story that *name is mud* refers to Dr. Samuel Mudd, the hapless Maryland physician who set John Wilkes Booth's leg after the assassination of Lincoln. The good doctor's name might have helped to popularize the expression in America, but it was current in Europe over three centuries before. It arose during the Italian Renaissance, when family rivalries were at a fever pitch, and when coats of arms—those symbolic "names"—were prominently displayed at the entrances to aristocratic families' homes. Fred Bryson, in his *Points of Honor in Sixteenth-Century Italy*, notes that, given the delicate sensibilities of that time, even passing in front of a rival family's house could be interpreted as "giving the insult." A more brazen, and unmistakable, method of doing so would be to perform an offensive act (*atto offensivo*) at the gate. Among the most popular of these acts was besmirching the coat of arms with mud. If the family whose coat of arms had been splattered with mud failed to retaliate promptly enough, it was said that it had acquired a *nome fangoso*, or "muddy name." Like all Italian Renaissance forms of insult, this ritualized form of mudslinging was described in Vitelloni's classic 1532 boor's handbook, *Il Manuale Maschio*, and reached the English-speaking world in Foxpaw's 1537 translation, *The True Man's Vade Mecum, or The Manly Arte of Giving Offense*. (See VITTLES.)

Mugging

The two basic meanings of this word are historically, though not clearly, related. The initial meaning of *mug* was simply "face," and *to mug* meant to "make a funny face," that is, to distort the mug for humorous purposes. So the first muggers were children and clowns. In the early 1900s, when the American Halloween was taking hold, the term was applied to the masked revelers who went door-to-door for trick or treat, since their "faces" too were distorted. The final step in the development toward the modern meaning came in the 1950s, when masked juvenile delinquents, especially under cover of Halloween, wreaked havoc on innocent strangers—not to mention their property—by demanding rather than asking for holiday "alms." Thus *mugging*, which was originally an innocent pleading, acquired the sense of robbery and assault.

Mumbo Jumbo

This colloquial equivalent for "gibberish" was a nineteenth-century British misconstruction of the West African formal greeting *mambo jambo*. The *mambo* part of this greeting survives in a debased form in the Caribbean, where it refers to a kind of ballroom dance. Originally, it meant "cosmic dance": It was the universal, divinely-ordered pattern that underlay all human affairs. *Jambo* meant "Hello" or "Good day," and it retains that meaning in Africa today. When a nineteenth-century African said "*Mambo jambo*," he was being highly formal and very friendly; an approximation of the phrase's meaning would have been "Welcome. I wish you good fortune in the universe's dance." Anglocentric explorers and missionaries missed this richness, giving us the mispronounced *mumbo jumbo* as a contemptuous dismissal of "native" speech.

Mum's the Word

Mum, or more properly *Mumm's*, was a rebel password during the Commune of Paris of 1871. Toward the end of that abortive experiment in revolutionary socialism, the communards, besieged by forces of the republican president Adolphe Thiers, were reduced to eating animals from the Paris zoo and to drinking water. Commune leaders, realizing that republican soldiers were aware of their privation, chose a password that evoked ruling-class elegance and that therefore, to defenders of that class, would have been inconceivable in the mouth of a communard: the name of Thiers's own favorite champagne, Mumm's. The choice did help to keep Commune plans from the ears of its attackers, but of course that did not save the enterprise. The last barricades were breached in May 1871, and 20,000 communards were executed. In a macabre, ironic twist, many of these were toasted by their executioners with champagne.

Cut the Mustard

Being unable to *cut the mustard* means that one's prowess is lacking. Both this basic meaning and the sexual connotation that the phrase often carries derive from the ancient Middle East. Centuries before Jesus used the mustard seed as a symbol for faith and for heaven, it was a symbol of masculine power, and as such it figured in a prenuptial ritual that was common from Mesopotamia to the Balkans. Making the same logical error that fueled the eugenics movement of later centuries, tribal elders equated martial and sexual accomplishments, and demanded that a groom-to-be prove his potential for fatherhood by demonstrating his skill with a sword. A mustard seed was placed on a chopping block, a blade was placed in the young hopeful's left hand, and he was instructed to *cut the mustard.* If he failed to split the tiny seed after three tries, he was deemed unworthy of marriage, and had to wait a year to try again.

Your Father's Mustache

In the ancient world, when male facial hair was an indication of age, wisdom, and honor, men frequently swore oaths by touching their chins and proclaiming "By my beard." Symbolically, this was a promise that, should the oath prove false, they could be shaven, like slaves were. To accuse someone of swearing by his mustache, and not his beard, was to suggest that his sincerity was less than complete, and to say that he swore by his father's mustache—thus putting the oath at two removes—was to impugn it entirely; for only a liar would find it necessary to swear by what the Sumerians called *khufi ta chakat,* or "someone else's false hair." Thus the expression *your father's mustache* has come down to us as an indication of mocking disbelief. Unfortunately, we have lost the more colorful Sumerian witticism *Khufi tama-tama redekh,* or "He lies by his grandmother's sideburns."

Naked as a Jaybird

Jaybird is usually taken as a colloquialism for *bluejay* or a corruption of *jailbird*, meaning prison inmate. Since neither usage implies nudity, the phrase *naked as a jaybird* demands further explanation. That explanation is found in the early history of Virginia, that rich expanse of unspoiled land and mild climate that so many English settlers likened to Eden.

One settler who found the resemblance to Eden particularly striking was a self-styled minister named Jason Byrd. Arriving in Chesapeake Bay in the 1640s, Byrd set up briefly as a fisherman, but soon turned his nets to catching men, and began preaching a doctrine he called "prelapserian purity" in the tiny settlements up and down the coast. The doctrine called for abolishing churches, rejecting the Trinity, and returning to the social structure of the first two chapters of Genesis. In particular, this meant the shedding of clothing, in accordance with the observation in Genesis. 2:25: "And they were both naked, the man and his wife, and were not ashamed." Byrd gathered a small band of followers around him before the tidewater clergy banished him, and with these converts he established the New World's first nudist colony in the foothills of the Appalachian Mountains. Defectors from the community carried salacious reports back to the coastal settlements, and the expression "naked as Jay Byrd" was born.

In the absence of archaeological remains, the fate of Byrd's colony is unknown. Most scholars believe that the prelapserians either starved to death in the mountains or intermarried with local Indians. Linguistic evidence supports the latter view: In the dialect of one Shenandoah tribe, *je-bedr-ta* is an affectionate form of address which means, approximately, "you crackpot without a loincloth."

In the Nick of Time

Until the advent of quartz-crystal and atomic clocks, the driving wheel of most timepieces was regulated by a mechanism called an escapement. An escapement consists of a ratcheted or "toothed" wheel and an arresting device called a pallet, which catches the teeth and allows them to "escape" at regular intervals; in many clocks the so-called ticking of the "gears" is actually the sound of the steady, periodic release of caught teeth. Horologists call these teeth "nicks," because when you view a ratcheted wheel head on, it seems to have been nicked around the perimeter. So to arrive somewhere "within a nick of time," in the fifteenth century, was to be within one "tooth" of a deadline.

Nine Days' Wonder

We call someone who is famous only for a brief, shining moment a *nine days' wonder* because nine days was the probationary period for medieval fools. Based on the standard period of reverence afforded patron saints, and thus called, like that period, a "novena," the nine-day trial period gave countless second-rate performers the opportunity to tickle the fancy of patron princes, although few of them, as might be expected, gained employment. The speed with which auditioning fools were thus turned over may be judged from an observation made by the Venerable Warhol, a scribe in the service of England's King John the Choosy. In his *Annales of a Reyne* he points out, "The juggling lott have so swiftly made theyre markes and thenn departed, that it seemeth likly, so favoreth it the Lord, that in future all vassales shalle bee wondrous for the space of this sayme nine dayes."

Dressed to the Nines

Nines here is often taken as a misrendering of the Anglo-Saxon *eyne*, for "eyes," so that to be *dressed to the nines* would mean to be bundled up to one's pupils. Since the expression indicates sartorial excellence rather than volume, this derivation is far-fetched. The phrase actually comes from the French, in which, colorfully but confusingly, *neuf* means both "nine" and "new." To *s'habiller de neuf* means to dress oneself up in new clothes; evidently it was a person unfamiliar with French idiom who first gave us the literal howler "to dress oneself to the nine."

Nitty-Gritty

Nitty-gritty today is usually used approvingly; when you "get down to the *nitty-gritty*," you are sensibly getting to the basics, or getting serious. A hundred years ago, when the phrase first appeared in England, it had the same sense of "basic," or "unadorned," but with a decidedly pejorative flavor. Nits are the eggs of head lice (hence *nit-picking* for close, meticulous work) and grit is, of course, fine sand. To "get down to nits and grits" was kitchen slang for discovering these unwelcome additions in your food. A *nitty-gritty* restaurant in that period was one that was known to be unsanitary, and where the basics of vermin constantly intruded. Cockney slang even spoke of "gritty spoons," in the same way that we speak of *greasy spoons*.

Nix

This slang equivalent of "no" originated in London just after World War II, when the city's characteristic double-decker buses were just being introduced into the urban transport scheme. At that germinal stage of the busing system, transfer arrangements from line to line had not yet been fully worked out. To avoid having passengers wait unnecessarily at single-line stations, the transport authority posted large "No Exchange" signs at those stops. To make the signs easier to see from a moving bus, the authority adopted a large, two-letter logo: NX. Thus "NX," which Londoners pronounced *nix*, acquired its current sense of negation.

Nose to the Grindstone

Eleanor Hodgman Porter's 1913 novel *Pollyanna* was one of the smash hits of the Edwardian Age, but not everyone was equally enamored of its doggedly optimistic heroine. A dyspeptic New Jersey librarian named Myrtyl Mason was so put off by Pollyanna's search for the silver lining behind every cloud that she penned a spoof called *Mollyanna*, published, appropriately, in the first year of World War I. Mason's story—which has been compared to the Book of Job, *Candide*, and Orwell's *1984*—was set in the mythical country of Travail. Its government was a model of totalitarian impartiality: "It oppressed all its citizens just the same." Pleasure in Travail was forbidden, because it would detract from the society's single goal: the achievement of "the Highest Standard of Living in the Known World"—and this included the simplest pleasures of the senses. Travailians were expected to be oblivious to the delights of bird song and flowers, sunshine and wine, and an elaborate system of penalties was in place to ensure that they remained free of temptation. A worker caught looking at a rainbow, for example, might be forced to work blindfolded for several days. Listening to music would get your earlobes snipped. In the most celebrated of Mason's grotesque revenges, a worker caught sniffing flowers might be reminded of the importance of constant labor by having his nose put literally to a grindstone. This not only provided a strong disincentive to that worker from ever "abusing" his nostrils again, but it also gave an unmistakable warning to others. The expression *as plain as the nose on your face* first appeared in Mason's dystopian novel, to describe the all-too-obvious effects of this punishment.

Mason's heroine Mollyanna herself suffers the nose-grinding penalty after she succumbs to what she herself describes as "a quite naughty passion for daffodils." The lesson does nothing to quench her perkiness, however, and she remains as "Mollyannaish" as before. It is her steadfast devotion to good cheer, even after she has been forced to spend a month sleeping in a pigsty and subjected to the Travailians' unspeakable Honey Bee Torture, that lends the novel its dry, satiric edge.

In a Nutshell

The condensed, bare-bones version of an argument or statement is spoken of as being *in a nutshell* because of a medieval Arab jurist named Al Saaj'al. Renowned for the brevity of his briefs, Saaj'al was summoned by the caliph of Baghdad in 1143 to revise that city's overwritten and cumbersome legal code. He responded by thoroughly rewriting it according to a unique guiding principle: Each piece of legislation must be worded so that, when it was written down, the paper could be folded in a square that would fit completely within an almond shell. This extremely economical, "nutshell" approach to legal complexity horrified the more liberal jurists, as it continues to horrify their spiritual descendants—they call Saaj'al "the Arabian Draco." But it delighted the caliph, who was pleased to have his decision-making so simplified. For example, whereas before Saaj'al's reform the caliph had to read through four scrolls of particulars describing "Penalties Accruing to Perpetrators of Ocular Deprivation," now he could open the relevant almond shell and find, simply, "An eye for an eye." And the caliph was not alone. Popular opinion was with the code trimmer—so much so that his name, when brought to the West by Crusaders, was transformed into the English and French *sage.*

Nutty as a Fruitcake

The association of fruits and nuts with mental imbalance goes back to the early nineteenth century, when the absence of refrigeration and preservatives made the spoilage of foodstuffs not uncommon. Baked goods that contained fruits or vegetables seemed particularly prone to this hazard, and fruitcakes were the most susceptible of all. Frequently these spoiled items were "donated" by bakers to hospital charity wards and asylums—the idea evidently being that, since their occupants were already ill, tainted banana bread couldn't do them much harm. Modern research on pastry spoilage, however, suggests that a quite specific type of harm was wrought by this practice. In the Fall 1986 *Proceedings* of the London-based Potpourri Society, we read that "certain mind-altering resins" are typically released by putrefying starchy matter, and that the madness of many nineteenth-century asylum patients may have been aggravated, if not actually induced, by their ingestion of such foods. "It can hardly be incidental," the society claims, "that the constituent parts of fruit-and-nut loaves all became metaphors for madness during precisely that decade, 1830–1840, when the unloading of these foods to asylums reached its furthest extent."

The constituent parts that the society mentions include not only the expected fruits and nuts of fruitcake and banana bread, but also a surprising one: apples. In the 1830s and 1840s, to be "appled" meant exactly the same thing as to be *bananas.* We do not use the expression today is due to a typesetter's error. In the 1849 edition of Weed Jimson's *Dictionary of the English Tongue* (a standard reference throughout the rest of the century), the long list of comparative words for madness was supposed to have included *appled*; but, because of the inversion of two crucial letters, it came out being spelled *addled*.

Odds and Ends

This is a carpenter's term, indicating inferior or leftover wood. *Odds* are lengths of siding or planking which have been split irregularly by a saw, rather than being sheared off clean; their odd (that is, nonrectangular) shape makes them unsuitable for anything but piecing work. *Ends* are just that: the ends that are trimmed off a board when it is cut to a needed length, and which are too short to be useful themselves.

In Edward Michael Stokes's *History of American Lumbering*, we find that other popular expressions also come from the woodworker's milieu: "Dishonest lumberers in the old days would often sell loose, trimmed ends to the innocent, claiming that when the customer added up all their lengths, he would find that the contract had been fulfilled, since the agreed-upon total number of board feet had been delivered. This practice was known as putting a person *at loose ends*. If the buyer was particularly ignorant of wood, he might even be sold 'raw' or unseasoned boards; when someone bought a consignment of this useless material, he was said, quite accurately, to have gotten the *raw end of the deal*."

Off-Color

In nightclub acts between the world wars, colored spotlights were a popular new technology, but one that was not yet entirely under control. Performers with a penchant for tomfoolery were often able to get laughs at the lighting man's expense by darting out of the spot without warning and forcing him to find them in the dark. This was an especially popular sight gag among comedians whose material tended toward the risqué, for they could take the opportunity of being temporarily "unspotted" to dash off a quick racy line in the dark and then, once the spotlighter found them, adopt an expression of "Who, me?" Thus to be "off the color" or "out of the spot." The game of playing "tag" with the light man also led, briefly, to the paradoxical use of *spotless* to mean "filthy."

OK

Among eighteenth-century English lovers, *coo* was a term of endearment or assent. It came from the cooing of doves, which was taken to be a prelude to mating, and it survives in the modern Cockney expletive "Cor blimey," frequently uttered as a term of approval. In the days preceding the American Revolution, when patriots seized every opportunity to mock traditional British mores, an offshoot of the Sons of Liberty in Boston started what they called a "broken English" movement, proposing that Americans proudly mutilate the King's English "in any and all manners possible." The most popular manner they suggested, according to Ronald and Peck, was to move the initial consonant of a word to the end of the word and then pronounce it with the nonsense suffix *-ay*. In this system *king*, for example, became *ingkay*; *law* became *awlay*; and the lover's assent *coo* became *ookay*. With the late eighteenth-century vowel shift, this became *okay* and then, by a process of false acronymization, *OK*.

Other "broken English" innovations failed to survive the victory at Yorktown, but the consonant-shift-plus-suffix device passed into children's speech and then into general folk usage. Because the Sons of Liberty had been failed Latin scholars, and because the gimmick had been used during the Revolution to confound British redcoats, or "pigs," it became known as *pig Latin*.

Paint the Town Red

During the ancient Roman Saturnalia—that annual display of public licentiousness which gave Rome its reputation for orgiastic behavior—not all the sports were carnal ones. Among the more sedate Saturnalian diversions was a game known as *simulacrum rubens*, which translates roughly as "red statue." Rival bands of youths would wander the streets, competing with each other to see who could drench the most marble statues with red wine. The entertainment was particularly popular during the consulship of Cicero, who noted in a recently discovered letter that effigies of Bacchus, for obvious reasons, were singled out most often for this honor. Because the porous marble frequently kept the tint of the *tinto* for some time after the festival, the youths were said, literally enough, to have *painted the town red*. Gradually this expression came to be applied not just to the revelries of Saturnalia, but to high-spirited "nights out" in general.

Panhandler

Settlers on the American frontier, having no access to permanent stores, relied on traveling peddlers for household supplies. These enterprising eccentrics stocked their wagons with everything from axle grease to window glass and adorned the sides of the vehicles with kitchen goods; not only did this save space, but the clattering of pots and pans announced their coming. Hence the nineteenth-century synonyms for peddler: *pot merchant, skilleteer,* and *panhandler.* The latter expression acquired its current meaning of "beggar" just after the end of the Civil War. It was a tendentious, and quite unfounded, connotation invented by newly established shop owners who wished the public to associate their nomadic competitors with penury and dependence— so that they could do the pan handling themselves.

Paper Tiger

A *paper tiger*, as the phrase implies, is a posturing aggressor without bite—in other words, a mere "paper" threat. When Mao Tse-tung called the American nuclear arsenal a *paper tiger* back in the 1960s, he was better understood in China than in the United States, for *paper tiger* is an old Chinese term—one with an amusing history. It arose during British penetration into the East in the middle of the last century, that HEYDAY of imperial expansion which was more warmly applauded along the Thames than along the Ganges and Yangtze. Between British entry into China in the 1830s and the country's capitulation to the Treaty of Tientsin in 1858, Chinese youths twitted the occupying army with a variety of pseudo-military "attacks." One popular trick was to position life-sized paintings of tigers on the perimeter of a sleeping encampment and then to alert the night watch with frenzied screams of "Help! Murder! Tiger!" In their confusion and fear, many young guards riddled these paper beasts with rifle fire before they discovered their mistake, while the painters enjoyed the joke from yards away.

Most of these original *paper tigers* were retrieved and destroyed by the British, but a few were recaptured by the young jokers. To snatch a bullet-vented painting away from the camp was a dangerous bit of adolescent heroism, and those who could accomplish this without themselves being shot were considered

almost mystically immune to subsequent injury. The retrieved paintings themselves also had power. Banned by the British in 1861, they were sold on the black market for years as simultaneously patriotic and protective icons. Many of them surfaced as fighting banners during the Boxer Uprising of 1900, and it is probably not accidental that Tiger Balm—the "miracle-working" salve still sold in health stores today—first surfaced at the same time. According to one Chinese legend, the original Tiger Balm's potency came from the fact that its secret ingredient was the paint—scraped off, melted down, and mixed with camphor—of the original *paper tigers*. (See also WRONG SIDE OF THE BED.)

Passing the Buck

When Egypt was under the colonial administration of Great Britain, many village leaders, resisting the blandishments of Anglo-Saxon law, held to traditional forms of adjudication, among them the settlement of disputes by means of round-table discussion and consensus. At these "court" gatherings, parliamentary procedure had no place. When someone wished to address the assembly, he asked to be handed a small, carved scarab, an ancient Egyptian emblem of the sun's divinity. With the scarab in front of him, he was bound to speak nothing but the truth, and he had the floor until he wished to relinquish it. He did that by moving the beetle-shaped symbol of "true words" in front of the next speaker who wanted it. It was this transfer of veracity that English observers contemptuously called "passing the bug." They had forgotten, evidently, that in the original Anglo-Saxon assembly, a similar procedure had been followed as a way of muting the contentiousness of the British tribes (see MAD AS A WET HEN). Eventually, in America, the original *bug* became a *buck*, and passing it came to be an image not just for relinquishing the right to speak, but for actively avoiding responsibility.

Pat on the Back

It is ironic that *pat on the back* today implies simple, straight-forward congratulations, for it was originally a precaution against danger. Among the ancient Greeks, one of the hazardous attitudes into which a human being could fall was the condition known as *hubris*, or excessive pride. A person afflicted with *hubris* was almost certainly bound for a fall, for the goddess Nemesis could not abide a haughty soul, and would cut it down as soon as it appeared. It was to guard against Nemesis that the Greeks patted each other on the back. The gesture reminded the person who was due for congratulations that he could always be struck down from behind, and that he should therefore be wary of boasting.

Stand Pat

To *stand pat* in draw poker is to keep your original five-card hand rather than attempting to better it by exchanges. The use of *pat* is a vestige of a poker-inspired novelty game that was popular in the 1920s along the Eastern Seaboard. It was called Charades Poker from New Jersey up to Boston, and Poker Charades between Philadelphia and Baltimore. Under either name, the rules were the same. Players of the game were pledged to silence, and had to indicate their betting and card-draw choices by means of gestures. To open betting, for example, a player would place his chips in the pot while opening his mouth in a wide yawn. To raise a bet, he would snap to military attention, salute the table, and mimic the raising of a flag up a pole. To ask for cards, he would run once around the table for every one he wanted. And to stick with his original dealt hand, he would rise to his feet and loudly pat his stomach, to show he was already "full." Hence "stand and pat" for staying where you are.

Charades Poker enjoyed a vogue for several seasons, although it was universally condemned by poker veterans. It really only fell out of favor during the early Depression, when the CP Clubs that enthusiasts had established were confused by local police with Communist Party (CP) cells. In Philadelphia especially, police raids took a toll on the game, and the last club there closed in 1933. Rex Beefheart, that city's eminent historian of fads, claims that the attack on Charades Poker was "as inimitably tendentious in its own way as Richard Nixon's confusion, a decade later, of the Boys' Clubs with W. E. B. Du Bois."

Patsy

The homeland of Europe's wandering gypsy bands was the plains of central and southern India, and it was there, before they began their long diaspora around the tenth century, that the gypsies gave rise to our term *patsy*, meaning someone who is easily deluded. In India the gypsies were known as *pa'tsulees* since they were fond of wearing *pa'tsul*, or patchouli oil, in their hair. They were also fond of the thievery which led them to be driven into the West, and the traditional Sanskrit term for "deceiver" or "con man" is a contraction of *patchouli*: *pa'tsee*. So a *patsy* was originally the person who was doing the taking, not the person taken in. It came to be applied to the object of the deception by a process that linguists call "denominational transmogrification," or the switching of object and subject. The process is common in the language of insult; compare the English noun *jerk*, for someone who is "jerked around"; and the German-influenced DORK, for someone who is "*durch*ed" over.

Take Down a Peg

Regular customers in the more traditional British pubs keep their own beer mugs behind the bar. This custom, which saves on glassware and provides a personal touch to the service, derives from the Restoration period, when customers' pewter tankards would hang above the bar, their handles looped over pegs. The arrangement of tankards on the "peg line" was entirely up to the landlord, although the general rule was one of convenience: The pegs that were closest to the tap would hold the tankards of his most frequent patrons. To have him move your tankard "down" the peg line—that is, away from the tap—meant you had fallen in his favor. Either because of the infrequency of your visits or because of personal disaffection, he no longer considered you important enough to merit his immediate attention. Thus to *take* someone down a peg (or two) was to puncture his sense of self-importance.

For Pete's Sake

This casual expression was once a sacred oath: One swore soberly to accomplish a certain task for the love of, or for the sake of, a holy Peter. As to the identity of this person, the obvious guess—Saint Peter—is not the right one. Peter is a corrupt form of the Latin word *pater*, meaning "father." To swear "by Peter" was thus the most solemn of all oaths: It was to swear by God the Father.

The alternate explanations that have been given for this phrase are fascinatingly wrong-headed. Erotologist George Alexander, with his customary smutty acumen, suggests a phallic origin, supposing that *peteromony*, or swearing by the phallus, was once as common as *testimony*, or swearing by the testicles. Squab claims that *Pete* was a common nickname for village idiots in nineteenth-century England, and suggests that alms were collected in his name. German scholars tend toward Peter Schlemihl, the well-meaning *schlemiel* of Yiddish folklore who, like the village idiot, would have to be taken care of by the community. All of these guesses, and more, are discredited in Gavotte and Mazurka's brilliant survey of European folk exclamations, *From Abbadabbadoo to Zounds*.

Peter Out

Because *peter* is a slang term for "penis," it has been suggested that *peter out*, meaning to diminish gradually, refers to diminishing urination. This engaging idea falls down on the basis of dating. According to Eric Partridge, the verb *peter* meant "to cease doing" as early as 1812, but the association with the penis did not come about until a generation later. So we must look elsewhere for an origin, and I would suggest Mark 14:66–72. That is where the apostle Peter, fearful of being arrested himself on the eve of the crucifixion, thrice denies knowledge of his friend Jesus. Clearly, it is the first pope's waning enthusiasm that provides the historical model for *petering out*.

In a Pig's Eye

This dismissive expression indicating unlikeliness (as in "Close all tax loopholes? *In a pig's eye!*") comes from the Roaring Twenties. Illegal saloons in that era were known first as speakeasies, because you had to speak softly, or "easy," to get in, and later as "blind pigs"—only God and Senator Volstead knew why. The typical speakeasy door contained a peephole through which the doorman could ascertain whether the people seeking admittance were known customers, strangers, or police. When a stranger made an appearance opposite one of these blind pigs' "eyes," the doorkeeper's judgment would be tested. He could admit the person, gambling that he was neither a brawler nor an officer of the law in disguise. Or he could play it safe and refuse admittance, claiming that the establishment was a private club.

To afford protection to the owners, many speakeasies did function as private clubs, and because their doormen were so rigorous in keeping out unknown elements, the expression "getting through the blind pig's eye" came to stand, among hard-drinking nonmembers, as a secular equivalent of "passing through the eye of the needle." Gradually the phrase was cut down to essentials, and *in a pig's eye* came to be a tag for any activity that was not likely to happen.

Take the Plunge

This metaphor for getting married recalls a prewedding ceremony of the Shoshone Indians. Among those people until almost the beginning of this century, before two lovers could be wed, they would have to walk together to a rock ledge and leap from it into a river below. If they trusted each other enough to perform this mutual feat, and if the spirits of the rock and the river permitted them to survive, they were deemed suited to become husband and wife. If they faltered or did not survive the plunge, they were considered, ipso facto, unmarriageable.

The expression *taking the plunge* reached Eastern ears through Adriana Martins's popular 1886 romance, *Catherine of Oregon*. A semiautobiographical tale based on the author's three-year captivity among the Shoshone, the novel was strongly pro-Indian, and was much praised by the same liberal readers who had made Helen Hunt Jackson's *Ramona* a bestseller two years before. Although somewhat less popular than that work, *Catherine* did include telling images. The plunge motif, for example, appeared in a chapter entitled "Lovers' Leap," which gave readers a memorable, if somewhat erroneous, view of doomed love. The book also popularized the supposedly generic Indian greeting *How*, which Martins claimed was a Shoshone contraction for "How pleasantly the Great Spirit's sun is shining on your most welcome face." And of course the story-in-song of Running Bear and Little White Dove—included in an interlude called "Tales of Passion"—became so deeply imbedded in American popular culture that halfway into the twentieth century it was recorded as a rock 'n' roll novelty tune.

Purple Prose

In ancient times the color purple was associated with public esteem and high rank. In Rome it was the shade of imperial robes, and in Greece the sign of kings and military leaders. Hence the expression *purple prose* for speech distinguished by rhetorical flourishes: This was the kind of speech that was appropriate not only to the high government officials, but also to anyone addressing them. The modern connotation of profanity came in only a century ago, when pornographic works in Victorian England were frequently printed on violet paper or in violet ink. It is not certain where this practice got started, although Squab makes the reasonable guess that the first book of "purple" porn was the 1881 *Story of V.* In this prurient little tale the heroine Violet not only speaks but also dresses all in purple.

Right as Rain

This expression is a relic of monarch worship or, in the legalistic phrasing of medieval Europe, of the "divine right of kings." Before seventeenth-century proto-liberals disabused them of the notion, the hereditary rulers of many Western kingdoms believed that they held their thrones from God; conveniently, this made them His legates on earth and meant that they could do no wrong. In England, therefore, the "King's will"—arbitrary and capricious as it may have been—had the same force as written law. In France as late as the eighteenth century, Louis XIV could say without fear of public denial, "*L'état, c'est moi.*" And in Spain during the tenure of Ferdinand and Isabella, the enlightened despots who sent Columbus to the Indies, a common way of applauding a person's righteousness was to say he was *tan recto como reina*, or "as correct as the queen." English privateers picked the phrase up from Spanish captives, and used it in a punning form to mock Iberian absolutism: "right as the *reina*" became the mundane *right as rain.*

Raining Cats and Dogs

In their fascinating survey of the unexplained, *Phenomena*, John Mitchell and Robert Rickard discuss numerous "frog and fish showers" that have been observed in Europe since ancient times.

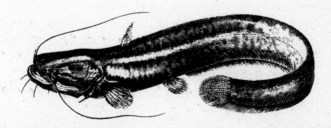

Explanations have ranged from the medieval conjecture that frogs "exist spermatically in the soil" waiting to "spring up with a shower of rain" to the marginally less ludicrous notions that the creatures fall from whirlwinds or vomiting birds. No clear conclusion can be drawn, but what does seem clear is that *cats* and *dogs* in the expression *raining cats and dogs* refer not to mammals but to fish—specifically the catfish and dogfish that an especially heavy rain might bring down.

Proof of the catfish link is found in Singapore. During an 1861 torrent there, Mitchell and Rickard note, fifty acres of land were found "covered with a local species of catfish." For the dogfish there is the evidence of folklore. The dogfish (it's actually a tiny predator called the salmon shark) has been considered a pest by North Atlantic fishermen for centuries, because its spiky dorsal fin can impart a painful wound. The Newfoundland proverb "Dogs at morning, trawler's warning" refers to an old sailors' belief that if dogfish were sighted on a morning run, a storm would come before noon—and the clouds of the storm would contain the fish.

Raspberry

A *raspberry* is the insulting, crepitous sound produced when you blow out through a stuck-out tongue. It is also called a *Bronx cheer*, and this is appropriate because it was invented in the Bronx, by a young ball player named Doyle Raspberry. A contemporary of Harvey Bunte (see BUNT), Raspberry played center field for the Bronx Oilers, and was equally well known for stupendous running catches and for dropping the easiest of pop flies. It is uncertain whether his concentration was simply uneven or whether he suffered from manic depression; the latter theory is put forth by Link Storm, in his biography of the center fielder *Raspberry, Shmazzberry, Catch the Ball*. Whatever the cause, Raspberry's erratic performance did not endear him to the fans, and they frequently pelted him with bottles. During one bottle storm in 1919, Raspberry suddenly turned toward the bleachers, put his hands to his ears in a gesture which is often called the Antler Sneer, and gave the world its first official *raspberry*. He repeated the feat on numerous other occasions, until gradually the fans responded in kind, and the traditional *Bronx cheer* was born. "This was not entirely a bad thing," Storm wrote. "In a sense, Raspberry civilized the game, by giving folks an alternative to the bottles."

In the Red/In the Black

It is widely understood that these terms come from the accountant's practice of showing overdrawn or other debit figures in red ink to make them more easily identifiable. What is not so commonly known is that this custom reflects the antagonism between church and state in the England of Henry VIII. Monastic ledger books were typically drawn in black ink in those days, as were ecclesiastical calendars. But liturgical holy days on the calendar were always distinguished by red ink; hence the term *red-letter day*. Because red was thus associated with religion, wealthy monasteries in Henry's reign began to show their tax deficits in red ink, the idea being that government inspectors had no right to question the deficit entries because they were entered in "God's" color. Thus they could be perennially *in the red* without having to answer to the Crown. It was just this type of accounting irregularity that caused Henry, in 1536, to mount his attack on monastic privilege, and to send special inspectors (see DODGE THE ISSUE) to set things right.

Red Herring

Chauncey "Red" Herring was an attorney whose career, the Culdesacks argue convincingly, gave us the term *Philadelphia lawyer*, meaning "shyster." Born in the City of Brotherly Love just after the end of the Civil War, Herring determined at an early age to follow the law and soon became adept at the glibness he believed essential to success. In his autobiography he tells us that "by seven I had made my first million, in marbles, just by talking the other chaps into surrendering them." By seventeen he had entered the university law school, and before twenty he was admitted to the bar. Herring made a career out of "defending the undefendable," including robber barons who had clearly watered stock and politicians caught with their hands in the till. The rarity of fraud and malfeasance convictions in Philadelphia during the Gilded Age has been laid directly at his door. He also seems to have initiated the idea of the contingency fee: After winning a thousand-dollar judgment in 1891 against a merchant who had slandered his client, Herring pocketed, as he tells us without shame, "my rightful share of 500 clams."

But it was as a defense lawyer that Herring made his reputation, and a principal reason for his success in this field was that he had, as he put it, "a tin ear for the opposite side's objections." This was his way of saying that whatever facts the opposition might bring up, he was an expert at obscuring them from the jury. He did this chiefly by the tactic which made his name a byword: presenting his own colorful facts that had nothing to do with the case. In his most celebrated case, for example, he defended a corrupt city official who, ten years before his indictment, had given a charitable contribution to an orphanage. Totally ignoring the prosecution's evidence that his client had reaped tax benefits from the action, Herring brought in a surprise witness, a young widow who said she had grown up in the orphanage and had been "saved by that good man's good deed." Weeping theatrically, she managed to make the jury completely forget the issue at hand: that the client had clearly stolen public funds. Herring's client got off, and the expression *a Red Herring* came to stand for a willful distraction.

Far from penitent about his misuse of the law, Herring boasted about it all his days, claiming it was the "whole point of advocacy" not to search for the truth but to "win the game." The title of his autobiography illustrates clearly how much stock he put in his own methods; referring to the "weeping widow" case, it was called *Crying Pays.*

Redneck

Being a *redneck* today is not nearly as racist a proposition as it once was. Thanks to the propaganda of Southern songwriters, redneckery is depicted as a benign blend of populism, hard work, good 'ol boy bonhomie, patriotism, and a mere whiff of nostalgia for the Old (that is, the segregated) South. This modern confection traces its roots, however, to the Klannish, lynch-ridden 1870s, when the Rednecks were a splinter group of the Klan distinguished by their public (that is, unmasked) defiance of the Reconstruction laws and by their wearing of the Confederate flag as a neckerchief. The red of the flag gave them their popular name; the official name was the White Anglo-Saxon Purity Society. Some authorities see the acronym WASP as a code version of this title.

Rib

Rib as an equivalent for "mock" or "jest" suggests the European practice of rib-elbowing as a gesture of humorous complicity. But in fact the practice followed the expression, and served to obscure an earlier practice. In ancient Britain, before the arrival of the Romans, to "rybbe" a person was to invite him to supper, and then to serve him the ribs of a venison roast which had been picked clean by the dogs. This custom, which dramatically flouted the Britons' high regard for hospitality, was never performed in front of strangers, but was confined to close family gatherings, where there was no danger of misinterpretation. The great British anthropologist Emmeline Squires, in her study *Domestic Politics of Rude Folk*, calls the practice a "comedic devaluation mechanism" by which the stringency of hospitality rules was ameliorated, and thus made more palatable to the hosts. The elbow-in-the-side practice, she claims, arose during the Roman occupation, as a way of disguising the original meaning: "True, the invaders viewed the public rib-nudging as a slightly ludicrous display; but to the form-conscious Anglo-Saxons, it was preferable to be mocked for eccentricity than to be exposed, even in jest, as questioning the inviolable host–guest bond."

Ringer

A *ringer* in sports parlance is an expert player hired by a mediocre team to give them an unpredictable advantage in a given game. Such ad hoc, technically illegal additions to the expected lineup have been used by sports teams for centuries, but they have only been called *ringers* for 100 years. The name is a reflection of the fact that, in the 1880s, when the telephone was just coming into popularity, such a player could be "rung up" and called in from a distant city.

The related term *dead ringer*, for someone who closely resembles another, is a political usage from the same period. National political candidates in the 1880s, not blessed with the advantages of the Lear jet and the yearlong campaign, frequently found themselves forced to skip stops on a two- or three-week campaign trail. The most harried candidates sometimes hired replacement speakers: "rung-up" stand-ins from their home districts who would dress up as the candidates and, in highly stylized performances, attempt to duplicate their messages and their appearances. It was an open secret that these speakers were merely *ringers* for the candidate. Nevertheless, in the spirit of fun-filled fidelity, they attempted to convince audiences of their stage identities, and the best of them were highly regarded as actors. *Dead* in this period meant "absolutely," as in the comment "You're dead right," and a *dead ringer* was a stand-in so convincing that voters could barely tell him from the real thing.

One of the most effective of these stump-speaking professionals was a New Jersey lawyer named Amos Jaspers. Jaspers campaigned for various Democratic candidates in the 1880s and 1890s, but was most memorable as a lookalike for Grover Cleveland, for whom he was "rung in" in the former president's 1893 bid for reelection. The lawyer mysteriously disappeared right after Cleveland's victory, and this led the more rabid anti-Clevelandites to claim that the president had had Jaspers murdered, lest his continued visibility confuse the public. Others claimed that our twenty-fourth president was in fact Jaspers and that Cleveland was the one who had disappeared. Other wild guesses about this curious episode in presidential history are covered in Winifred Buttons's book *Grover, Grover, Who's Got the Grover? A History of the Jaspers Affair*, published privately by the Amosite Memorial Society in 1910.

Rip Off

Rip off, both as a noun and as a verb, refers to swindling or related injustices, in which the person *ripped off* is the injured party. The expression was popular in the 1960s on American campuses, where it was most commonly used to denounce the (real or imagined) depradations of landlords, harsh graders, and government officials. As with many folk expressions, the first usage of the term is virtually untraceable, but folklorist Lulu Badger makes a reasonable guess as to origin in her "demythologized *socioeconozeitgeistliche*" survey of college slang, *It's Like Groovy, Y'Know?* "Berkeley and Michigan students," she writes, "were using *rip off* in 1968 and 1969, respectively, to characterize the onerousness of departmental requirements. In the winter of 1967, however, the term appeared in what I suspect was its *Ur*-form, at Cornell. On that equally political campus, the War had generated dozens of student factions, and all of these had to compete for limited announcement space on the campus center's bulletin boards. Frequently, rival groups would tear down each other's posters to make way for their own, and this practice came to be known as "ripping off *the opposition.*" The connotation of dishonesty, of course, was supplied by the groups so abused."

Off Your Rocker

Today the rocking chair is associated with the aged, but in the middle of the nineteenth century, when psychology was just bridging the gap between ancient superstition and modern hum-buggery, *rocker* suggested "mentally infirm." Physicians who had noticed the soothing effect of rocking on the elderly surmised that the chairs might also prove beneficial to their more obstreperous mental patients, and the chairs gradually became fixtures in asylums. Rocking chairs tranquilized problem cases at least as well as straightjackets and shackles, and only fell out of favor with the discovery of thorazine.

Rockers plus restraints were often used as "therapy" for violent cases, so that to be constantly on your rocker meant your prognosis for recovery was poor. When a violent patient broke his restraints and ran amok, he was said, literally enough, to be *off his rocker*, and it was from this technical description that the modern connotation derives.

The professional literature on rocking-chair therapy is limited but fascinating. I recommend particularly the work of linguist J.-J. Mallou, who shows that the French term *mal équilibré* (equivalent to our "unbalanced") originated in a Paris asylum

whose rocking chairs were inexpertly made; and that of th
ican scholar Mary Snipes, whose study of Charlotte Brontë
Rochester and Her Rocker," puts a whole new light on Jane
The suggestion, by Cal Tech geologist B. Q. Wiesbaden, tha
your rocker is a variation of "off the Richter scale," is not to
taken seriously.

Rolling in Dough

When hipsters of the 1940s spoke of money as "bread," they were
evoking a long English tradition: *bread dough* was a synonym
for "wealth" as long ago as the eleventh century. At a time when
bread was truly the staff of life for most people, there was simple
economic logic in this: a belly full of bread did mean affluence.
But there was a social aspect as well. In the east of England, and
especially in the Cambridgeshire wheat basket, the nobility used
to hold annual Dough Fairs at which the products of their bak-
eries were sold, but which also gave them an opportunity to show
off, by participating in "dough rolling" competitions.

The most famous of these competitions was held in July in the
Cantabrian barley capital, the town of Pilbury. There each noble's
baker would prepare dough beginning on the morning of the
competition, and starting around noon the nobles themselves
would be rolled in it until they were virtually turned into mammoth buns. Each noble was rolled only in his own baker's dough,
and at the end of the day, the hugest human bun was declared
the winner. By public acclaim he was granted an ad hoc title
(usually "Yeast King," sometimes "Pilbury Dough Boy"), and he
was expected to demonstrate his royal largess by picking off gobs
of the dough and flinging them generously to the crowd.

The meaning of these contests has been debated. Warren
Wright, in *More Strange Survivals*, sees it as a vestige of a primitive "eucharistic rite," in which the local king was baked and
eaten communally. Eric Quill, in his *Social History of Yeast*,

...at dough rolling was "a way to get
...have a good time besides." My own
...er authorities, is that the custom served
...chanism even as it applauded conspicuous
...d the nobility by encouraging their extrava-
...ch like the Feast of Fools ceremonies of the same
... HOLY MACKEREL), it allowed the common people to
...their betters in a safe, nonpolitical format.

Rotten Egg

The juvenile challenge "Last one in is a *rotten egg*" refers obliquely to the Norse epic *Rôtenaksdrápa*, dating from about the ninth century. The hero of the poem, the hunter Rôtenak, is depicted as brave but foolhardy. To win glory for himself and his clan, he takes chances that the gods consider excessive, and he dies as a boastful overreacher, unable to balance valor with wisdom. To demonstrate his courage, he allows one opponent, the dragon Merlhaggard, to bite off his head in a battle, and is recapitated only through the mercy of Freya. Freya rescues him again when, in an attempt to climb the great World Tree, he falls and breaks every bone in his body; the northern European phrase *pull oneself together* (for "control your passions") recalls the goddess's gathering together of Rôtenak's scattered bones after this second reckless adventure. She only gives up on the hunter when he chooses to show off on a Friday, by walking naked into the forest and announcing he will return in three days, unfazed by the iciest winds. Since Friday is of course "Freya's Day," the goddess takes this as a challenge to her power, and summons up a blizzard which freezes Rôtenak solid. Scandinavian parents still use this legend to warn their children against staying out too long in winter; the modern *rotten egg* expression is an Anglicized form of the old Swedish saying, "The last one in was Rôtenak."

Rube

This abbreviation of the proper name *Reuben* has meant "country bumpkin" since the late 1800s. Why *Reuben* should imply rusticness is uncertain, although the likeliest explanation is given by Norman Denker in his mammoth *History of the North Yellowstone Jews*. In spite of his untenable thesis that the American Indians were descended from the lost tribes of Israel (a popular Victorian delusion), Denker gives much useful information about Jewish settlements in the West, and about their unsteady relationship with gentile towns. In most of the western territories, he says, Jews tended to homestead far from town, partly, he acknowledges, out of clannishness and partly as a reaction to being snubbed. Gentile settlers, closer to town, looked down on them not only out of racism, but on account of their "backward, dirt-kicking ways." "Some of these Hebrew types," he quotes an 1898 Montana newspaper, "are no better than the Blackfeet (so perfectly named) or the Soo. I've seen them turn their noses up at bacon. No wonder God has given them the rocky ground." Since many of the "Hebrew types" were called Reuben, the name became a slur denoting backwardness, and ultimately a shorthand term for any country man.

Rule of Thumb

In the Middle Ages, when few rulers could sign their names, royal edicts were frequently "signed" with an X or with the monarch's fingerprints; hence the confusion in Old French between *regle du doigt* ("rule of the finger") and *regle du droit* ("rule of law"). In tenth-century France, during the reigns of Charles the Slow and his son Jean-Louis the Dropout, it was customary for legal announcements to carry anywhere from one to five fingerprints, depending on the law being passed. A five-finger signing was used for laws against capital crimes; four fingers for those against theft; and so on through the less grievous offenses. The least serious of crimes which would still merit royal attention were those violating the weights-and-measures laws (for example, short weighting by a baker) and these, being relatively minor, were itemized on documents bearing only a thumb print. Thus *rule of thumb* (*regle du pouce*) came to mean the kind of unwritten rule that measurers of various kinds—bakers, carpenters, surveyors—used in their daily work.

Scab

The insulting term *scab*, for a strikebreaker, sounds like mere egregious taunting: It seems to liken one who would cross a picket line to something familiar but disgusting. Actually, that's not the meaning. *Scab* is a mutilated form of Latin *sclavus*, from which we get *slave* and also *Slav*. (The Slavs were often slaves in ancient times.) It was first used on picket lines during the strike-torn 1880s, evidently by German-American factory workers who saw their jobs being taken by Eastern Europeans. Possibly these workers were classical scholars, but more likely they condemned the Slav immigrants, and the word came out sounding like *scab*.

Scoop

A *scop* in ancient Britain was a bard: one of those professional song-and-story men who, in the words of E. Cobham Brewer, "celebrated the deeds of the gods and heroes, incited to battle, acted as heralds, and sang at festivals." To the war chieftains of the fifth and sixth centuries, when bardic rhyme came to fruition, the first of these tasks was most important. Since a dead hero survived only in bardic tales, the scop's livelihood depended upon his skill in celebrating the deeds of warrior patrons. Naturally, after a given battle had been won, the first scop to come up with a laudatory lay would be more prized by the victor than his slower rivals: It was rapidity of fame, not literary style, that the chieftains wanted. This is why newspaper people, working on very much the same principle, speak of *scooping* their competition when they are the first to jump on a story.

The Whole Shebang

Irish gypsies, like most of their European counterparts, pursue their nomadic lifestyle in trailers or, as they are called in the British Isles, caravans. In the premotorized era, these traveling homes were drawn by horses, and in the Romany tongue (curiously close to the Gaelic in this instance) they were called *chev-anga*, or "horse buildings"; the English corrupted this into *shebang*. Since gypsies transported literally everything they owned in these vehicles, *the whole shebang* came to stand for completeness.

In an obviously facetious article entitled "Cinqs but No Cinqs" (in *Noodling Magazine*, Spring 1981), Tesla Gavotte suggests that *shebang* may be an "intensified" form of Indic *shang*, from which the French get their *cinq* ("five") and the English their *sink*. Gavotte refers to a "long-forgotten gypsy tradition" in which each encampment had to have five wells, or *shangs*, dug in a star-shaped pattern. The expression *everything but the kitchen sink*, he claims, is a mistranslation of Romany *huli kitcha shang*, or "Remember to fill in the wells," indicating the "completion" of an encampment. To those readers (and there are many) who have taken this silliness seriously, I can do no better than to quote a recent letter I received from Gavotte's brother: "Ca Tesla. Hoykavoki. Vatta kard."

Shenanigans

This is a compression of the Old Irish saying *Shee nanna gasne*, or "The Shee are rattling the dishes." The Shee, in Irish tradition, were the invisible fairy folk who ruled Ireland, at least unofficially, before the Christians came. Some of them, such as the banshee, were grim creatures: A banshee's wail often presaged death. But others were merely high-spirited: The leprechauns, a modern example, are a kind of village, stage-version of the breed. But even the mildest Shee were fond of mischief. Like poltergeists in the continental folk traditions, they were particularly fond of teaching Big People humility by shaking up their crockery and moving furniture. When tables swayed or windows flew open in an Irish cottage, the occupants typically muttered *Shee nanna gasne*, both as a greeting to the spirits and as a polite invitation for them to leave. The Culdesacks say that the shortened form of the invocation, *shenanigans*, had become a generalized synonym for "mischief" or "highjinks" by the middle of the eighteenth century.

On a Shoestring

This bit of Depression-era slang recalls the fact that, after the stock market crash wiped them out, many business people reentered the work force at the bottom, by hawking such common necessities as pencils and shoelaces on the street. Thus to start a business *on a shoestring* (or, for a couple of years in the mid-1930s, "on a pencil") was to begin it with virtually no capital. Interestingly, there was a Roman precedent for this. Freed slaves under the Empire were often given a start by their former masters by being given a *lori beneficium*, or "benefit of the thong." This meant that, along with their freedom, they were presented with a small supply of sandal thongs, or *lora*, which would enable them to set up as doorway vendors. The custom is reflected in the Latin metaphor for beginning a business career, *crepidam ponens in porta*, or "putting your sandal in the door."

Skedaddle

This colloquialism for "move along" or "hurry" is not, as Yarrowville absurdly maintains, a variation of Old Norse *skaelda*, for "sword"; his suggestion that "*skedaddle* was what you were forced to do if you were chased with a *skaelda*" is only one example among many of his reckless approach to etymology. The brilliant Russian linguist Boris Badinoff, in his cross-cultural masterpiece *Contractions I Have Known and Loved*, identifies the actual derivation: "*Skedaddle* comes from western Pennsylvania, where in the early 1800s it meant to run away quickly, particularly from danger. The original form was 'Let's get out of here,' and this was contracted, by 1820, first to *sgetouta* and then to *skedaddle*."

Skid Row

The original *Skid Row* was a short, winding street in Los Angeles (the city's name for it was Beverly Drive) which, in the words of an investigating commission that subjected it to "urban renewal" in 1938, was "ineptly graded, poorly lit, and badly marked." So many accidents and near-accidents had occurred along this strip that the pavement was completely blackened with tire marks—hence the nickname—and the place was a graveyard for abandoned cars. When migrants and hoboes began to use these vehicles as temporary shelters in the 1930s, Skid Row became a cause célèbre for local reformers and was exposed as a "national scandal" in *Life* and *Look* magazines. The people were moved out, a housing project was built on the site, and the expression *skid row* entered the language to describe any area with a large derelict population.

Skin a Cat

There may be many ways to *skin a cat* today, but in medieval England there were literally dozens. *Skin* at the time was a code word: it meant to skin, dress, and cook the animal. As Robert Darnton has shown in his wonderful book *The Great Cat Massacre*, eighteenth-century French laborers frequently tortured cats and even roasted them alive as a symbolic attack on their bourgeois owners. Much the same process had occurred in the north of England four centuries earlier—especially after the failure of the 1381 Peasants' Revolt, when popular resentment of the unbelled "royal cat," King Richard II, led to wholesale slaughter of wandering felines, and when food shortages gave these depradations an economic rationale. Many, if not most, of the cats killed by frustrated peasants eventually ended up in their stomachs, and so popular was cat as a main dish (in the north—but see HUMBLE PIE) that a 1399 "receipt book" contained an entire chapter on cat stews.

Cat eating was condemned by royal edict in 1384, since Richard was very much aware of the symbolic implications of his subjects' passion. Yet it continued in the north for a generation, with hungry peasants finding more and more ways to disguise the popular meat in a stew. It was in the early 1400s that the phrase "more than one way to *skin a cat*" took on its connotation of ingenuity, and in which the animal acquired its supposed *nine lives*: Among the most popular of the fifteenth-century obscurationist recipes was a mixture of one cat and nine chicken livers. Not surprisingly, this was also the period that gave us the term *nervous as a cat*.

It's a Snap

This has nothing to do with snapping fingers. It comes from Holland, where it was contemptuous shorthand for "It's only a snapdragon." In that country in the years 1634–1636, an outbreak of "tulipomania" so discombobulated the population that tulip speculators invested their entire savings in a single bulb, and committed suicide or left the country when the prices fell. The craze has been amply documented by Mackay in his *Popular Delusions*, and I will not repeat the details here. Suffice it to say that for those two years, tulip bulbs served the same purpose for the Dutch bourgeoisie that junk bonds and "surefire" gold stocks do now. Thus *It's a snap*, which now means "It's so easy," then meant "It's so easy to come by that it is not worth my money." Snapdragons were the bummer stocks of the day.

Snow Job

In the early, prestatehood days of Alaskan settlement, the country drew not only pioneers but also the usual crop of hangers-on and con men that always prey on the foolish along the frontier. Among the most successful of these parasites were the land speculators, and among every group of speculators there were always an unscrupulous few who specialized in *snow jobs*. Since Alaska lay under snow and ice for much of the year, the bona fide selling of real estate really only began in late spring, when potential buyers could inspect the thawed out land. "Snow jobbers," preying on the most ignorant new arrivals, would approach them in the dead of winter with "special deals." Displaying photographs and "recently assayed" soil samples supposedly from the snow-covered land, they would offer to unload "prime" spots at bargain rates if the buyer were willing to act now. Most of the people taken in by this ruse found, once the spring melt began, that they were the proud owners of marshland or solid granite—entirely unsuitable for herding or farming. *Snow job* was a trade description of this practice, and it soon came to mean any con.

Up to Snuff

This is an American PANHANDLERS' term dating from the bleak 1930s. Down-and-out men of that era reckoned the level of their distress with a euphemistic shorthand that reflected the price of tobacco. If you had money enough for a cigar, for example, you were said to be "stogie-rich." If you lacked the funds even for snuff—the cheapest form of tobacco—you were not *up to snuff*—that is, flat BROKE. The expression *up to snuff* survives today to describe anything minimally acceptable. For reasons I cannot understand, we have lost its more colorful cousins "up to chaw," "up to Lucky Strike," and "up to Prince Albert in the can."

Hit the Spot

This is a nightclub term dating from the 1920s. At that time the lighting techniques that had been developed by stagecrafters John and Anton Kliegl (inventors of the klieg light) were catching on not only in the theater, but in show business generally, and cabaret managers were using the brothers' narrow-beam, high-intensity "spot" lights to dramatize their performers' entrances. *The spot* was that point on the stage that would be sharply and instantly illuminated when the light man heard the orchestra's cue; ideally, the performer would "hit" that spot—walk to precisely the right position on the darkened stage—a second before the cue was given. Hence *hit the spot* for anything well executed or satisfying.

To put someone *on the spot*, incidentally, is police usage from the same era. In this variation, *the spot* was the chair in which a suspect would be interrogated. Like the stage spot, it would be brightly lit by one of the new Kliegl products. So to be put *on the spot* was to be intimidated by excessive scrutiny. (See also OFF-COLOR.)

On a Spree

The River Spree runs through the easternmost section of Germany (Lusatia), bisects Berlin, and then joins the Elbe to empty into the North Sea. In the eighteenth century, when Berlin was a bustling but somewhat sedate city, the country people who lived along the Spree—and especially in the Spree Forest, near Lübben—were notorious for their high-spirited licentiousness. The name Lübben itself is a variant of Lusatian *löben*, for "praise," and it refers to an ancient local ceremony in which songs of praise were sung to fleshly delights. For a Berliner to be *am Spree*, or "on the Spree," meant that he was experiencing those delights in one of the region's many legal brothels.

Star

The four great leading parts of the Italian commedia del l'arte were those of Pierrot the clown, Columbine the maiden, Scaramouche the braggart soldier, and Pantaleone the old geezer. In the sixteenth century, when this distinctive art form flourished, most Europeans were illiterate, and to identify the dressing rooms of these four principals for stagehands and costume ladies, Italian impresarios devised, around 1650, an ingenious visual code. On each player's door they tacked a paper cutout which could be easily remembered by those concerned, and which required no reading. By no particular design, a five-pointed star was chosen for Pierrot, a circle for Columbine, a crescent moon for Scaramouche, and a triangle for Pantaleone. Since Pierrot was by far the most popular character in the commedia, and since he had been assigned the paper *stella*, "stellar" or *star* qualities came to mean the qualities of this character's performance; to be the *star* meant to be Pierrot. If sixteenth-century Italians had been more enamored of the *miles gloriosus* type than they were of the white-faced clown, we might now be speaking of Robert Redford as one of Hollywood's most popular "moons."

Stir Crazy

It is commonly assumed that this phrase refers to the edginess of convicts in prison. It's true that *stir* has meant "prison" for centuries, and that it comes from the Saxon term for "punishment." But this explanation does not go far enough. The reason that prisons were called *stirs* in the first place is because that is what criminals did there. The Saxon equivalent of license-plate stamping was the tedious occupation known as *ealustyr*, or "ale stirring." As any home brewer can tell you, a pot of bubbling hops is heady stuff; stirring it for more than a few minutes will induce drowsiness and lightedheadedness in almost anyone. Therefore, so that freemen would not be incapacitated from doing their work, a Saxon community's ale was always brewed by convict or forced labor. To go *styrgemaed*, or "stir mad," meant you had spent too much time inhaling the fumes. This is also where we got *hopping mad*.

Keep One in Stitches

Many commentators have suggested that this phrase refers to an ancient superstition that, if a person laughed too loud or too long, he would literally "bust a gut" and have to be stitched up by a surgeon. Not true. Tesla Gavotte has shown convincingly that the expression first appeared with its current connotation around 1800 in American neighborhoods composed of Northern Europeans and more-recently arrived Slovaks. The Slovak for "stitch" is the cognate *stichy*, and to be "in stitches" to a Slovak meant to be in serious trouble: specifically, to be sewn up inside a sack. (Gavotte believes the expression reflects a medieval punishment for grain theft.) Americans from Northern European backgrounds found this visual metaphor so droll that the New World idiom acquired exactly the opposite connotation: to be "in stitches" or "all stitched up" meant that you had been told a patently ridiculous story—one to which the only appropriate response was laughter.

Pulling Out the Stops

A *stop* is an automobile speed governor, a device which safety enthusiasts began to promote in the 1940s as a way of regulating highway speeds and reducing accidents. Since these devices "govern" the machine's speed automatically—by cutting the gas feed when the car reaches a certain speed—they were never very popular with motorists, and Americans who believe that highway mayhem is a constitutional right have always considered them threatening to personal liberty. Nor has it ever been easy to have such governors implanted permanently in the car; any novice mechanic can remove them. This is just what happened, in fact, when governor-equipped cars were marketed briefly in the first days of Ralph Nader's influence. That is when we got *pulling out the stops* as an equivalent of "going all out" or "getting up to speed."

Straight Up

Hard liquor that is served without the addition of ice or mixer is said to be presented *straight up*. The *straight* part is straightforward enough, but why *up*? The answer is that, in the Old West, as many Hollywood Westerns remind us, cowboys in from the trail would often order their firewater by the bottle. The bottle itself remained upright on the drinker's table even after he had fallen under it, and it is from this fact that the expression probably arose. Rance Bozeman claims, however, that the term was a shortening of "straight upside down." In *Trail Gossip* he notes that many cowboy drinkers, not wanting to waste time with pouring, gulped their redeye directly from the bottle: "They'd tip that old soldier straight up, and the HOOCH would run down like burning rain. Only way to drink, O'Malley says. I recollect the time he saw some traders, out Kearny way, drinking tin cups of whiskey and water. Them are the kind of sissy boys, he says to me, go crying for their mittens at five below."

Straw Man

A *straw man* today is an idea that is introduced into an argument for no other purpose than to be knocked down. The original *straw men* served exactly the same function. They were the bayonet-practice dummies that the Germans invented in the 1860s, just in time for the American Civil War, and that the French adopted just before the Franco-Prussian War. The French call such a dummy an *homme de paille*; we get our word from the German *Strohmann*.

Play Out a String

Ronald and Peck think that *string* here means "string of horses," and that *play out a string* was a cowboys' term meaning to go through a herd, one by one, selecting each mount in turn on a circular basis until the entire herd had been ridden or *played out.* Possible, but I think a better guess is Jesse Rinaldo's. In his *Universal History of Noncontact Sports*, he says that the phrase suggests a kite string, which the kiter feeds or *plays out* to its full length. Folkloric and linguistic support for the kite theory comes from the fact that, as Rinaldo puts it, "the kite-maddened province of Lower Catalonia was the source not only for this seventeenth-century expression but also for *cabo de cordel*, which we know as *end of one's rope* but that the Spanish took as "end of one's string."

Stuffed Shirt

This image of pretension and pomposity comes from the Congo region of central Africa, where nineteenth-century colonialists found numerous villages run by headmen who cultivated ostentatiously large paunches. In this they were similar to their European and American counterparts, for whom fatness was also a sign of social status (see, for example, FAT CAT). But to enhance their dignity in the eyes of their communities, many of the African leaders resorted to a tactic unknown in the West: They placed yams and other bulky foodstuffs over their stomachs inside their clothing. The custom was not really intended to fool anyone, but only to demonstrate that the owners of the protruding bellies *could* eat that much food if they wanted. This subtlety was lost on European observers, who brought *stuffed shirt* back to their homelands to describe anybody PUTTING ON AIRS.

Suck an Egg

"Go suck an egg" sounds today like a pointless, arbitrary taunt, but in Elizabethan times, when it was far more common, it had a specific medical meaning. Renaissance "physicke books" nearly all agreed that the albumen of an uncooked egg was useful both to stanch running blood and as a purgative for "inner blood," that is, irascibility or anger. Thus Wrexham's 1592 manual *Remedies Herballe and Otherwyse* counsels, "When that ye shall bleed, eyther from the skinne or thy spleyne, stop upp the violent swell with the raw jelly of an egge." And, in Violete Balinwoke's survey of Leicestershire folk cures, published in 1613, we find that eggwhite is recommended as "a verry parfit unmaker of vile wroth, when it bee sucked from the shell." Chicken eggs were quite suitable for this purpose, but the eggs of wild fowl such as Guinea hens seem to have been most highly prized— Wrexham says because "the wildeness of the orbe doth serve to assuage the wildeness of the person afflicted, by the principalle of *similia similibus*." So when an Elizabethan told an acquaintance to suck an egg, he was advising him to dampen his aggravation. Eggwhite was the valium of its day.

Swank

District administrators in British India were commonly called *nawbobs* or *nabobs,* from the Urdu word *nauwob*, meaning "governor." In time *nabob* came to mean any person of high social standing, and this led to the terms *swank* and *swanky*, pertaining to the lifestyle of such persons. The original spelling of *swank* was with a C: it was the acronym S.W.A.N.C., for the South West Asia Nabob's Club, situated in the Punjab just north of Delhi. This private club, founded in 1790, catered to British officers and their ladies, and was notorious among the poor for its ostentation: No less than a hundred elephants had given their tusks, for example, to provide a framework for its massive central bar. Not surprisingly, the Sepoy mutineers of 1857 burned the hated symbol to the ground, leaving only the designation "swanc" as a reminder of imperial excess. (For more on *nabobs*, see WHOLE NINE YARDS.)

Don't Sweat It

The American Indians used "sweat lodges" for a variety of purposes. The two most widely remembered are probably health and religion: People would enter a sweat lodge to purify the pores or the soul. But the lodges were also used for more mundane purposes, and on the Appalachian frontier, where the expression *Don't sweat it* arose around 1750, one of these purposes was "venting the troubles" or, as we would put it today, sulking. It was believed that bad feelings, particularly jealousy and anger, could be driven from the body by means of sweat, and indeed the word *sulking* itself is a frontier variant of *soaking.* So when an eighteenth-century American said *Don't sweat it*, what he meant was "Don't get so upset that you will have to retreat to a lodge."

Done to a T

This is a cabinetmakers' term indicating a high degree of regularity. The reference is to the carpenter's T-square, a ruler with a right-angled crosspiece that is used to maintain the rectangularity of a construction. A piece of work, whether a bookcase or a building, whose angles fit the T-square exactly was said to be done, or finished, "to the T." It was also spoken of as being "done square" or "made on the square;" it is from these latter expressions that we get the modern term *square* for "upright" or "honest." Interestingly, the adolescent insult *square*—meaning "unhip" or "not in the know"—also comes, indirectly, from this source. In this sense, the term was first used by jazz musicians in the 1940s, to deride other musicians who could not appreciate the eccentric fluidity of the bebop style—that is, those who liked their music laid out in boring, predictable, squared lines.

Take It Easy

The first people to say *take it easy* when they meant "Relax" were the members of the British Army's bomb squads, during the tense days of the London blitz. The principal job of that courageous band was to defuse delayed-action or ostensibly "dud" German bombs that were lying, ready to explode, in the city rubble. Most of these bombs were what the Germans themselves called *Bübenstücken*, which means literally "boy's pieces" but which carries the idiomatic sense of "mischief" or "prank," and which the bomb experts translated as "booby pieces"—changed, once their lethal characteristics became known, into *booby traps*. Neutralizing these traps involved removing the detonator from its housing without jostling the device; so taking it (the detonator) out easy—in a slow, relaxed manner—became a prerequisite for survival.

Third Degree

To give a crime suspect the *third degree* is to subject him to rigorous interrogation, or *grilling* (see HOT SEAT). The term dates from the fifteenth century, when under the hand of the first Grand Inquisitor, Torquemada, the Spanish Inquisition reached the height of its power. Established in 1478 to verify the sincerity of Jewish and Muslim converts to the Church, this ecclesiastical authority was empowered by the state to use any and all means, including torture, to ensure that the Faith was not contaminated by false believers. One of the most popular torture methods was the Italian import known as the *strappado*, and it is from this grotesque practice that we get the expression *third degree*.

Strappare in Italian means "to tear off," and the *strappado* tore off the victim's arms—or, more precisely, dislocated them from the shoulders. Inquisition regulations stipulated three degrees, or *grados*, to the torture. In the first, the victim's arms were tied behind his back at the waist, a long cord was tied to his wrists, and he was hoisted off the ground by means of a pulley, so that his body weight pulled his arms up and backward. If he failed to confess at this point, the torturers would increase the pressure by tying heavy weights to his ankles; this was the second degree. If he still maintained his innocence, they would raise the weighted body toward the ceiling and then allow it to drop abruptly to its original position—a practice which virtually ensured dislocation and lifetime crippling. It was this final, wrenching exercise in ecclesiastical paranoia that was known as the *tercero grado*, or *third degree*.

Thumb One's Nose

It's an old folk insult to push one's thumb up into one's nostril, thus raising the *nose in the air*, to indicate disdain for another.

Desmond Morris and other sociobiologists, who identify this extremely rude gesture as a mimetic, formalized suggestion of "snot-flicking," have called it by far the most common of all European insult gestures, prevalent from Birmingham to the Balkans. They do not explain, however, why it should be so common a sign of contempt.

The answer to that puzzling question is found in Paul D. Paul's fascinating survey of European humor about "unmentionables," *The Surprising History of Excreta.* Paul writes that among the ancient Europeans, as among many primitive peoples, "detached body parts such as fingernails, hair, and mucus" were considered both magical and dangerous: If they fell into the wrong hands, they could be used to work their owners' ill. Thus many peoples hid or buried their excreta, away from the eyes of potential enemies. For someone to hurl snot in another's direction was an insult not because mucus was inherently disgusting but because, by doing so, the hurler was showing fearlessness. The message was this: You are so insignificant a person that I do not mind giving this advantage; your magic is too weak to harm me. There is some evidence, Paul notes, that among the Gallic tribes of the pre-Roman era, contempt could also be shown by shaking dandruff in a despised person's direction. "Dandruff was then known as "snow," and the Old Frankish phrase *je to-naja*, or 'I snow on you,' was tantamount to a challenge to duel."

One more modern twist on the nose-thumbing practice was added by Italian insult expert Girolamo Vitelloni (see VITTLES) in his 1532 insult manual. To those seeking ever more novel ways of offending others, Vitelloni advised performing the snot-flicking gesture not with the thumb but with the middle finger. "It doth provide more distance and greater accuracie," according to the English version of his text. Our expression *giving one the finger*, although it has by now acquired phallic connotations, can be traced back directly to the Italian innovation.

Steal One's Thunder

It is frequently observed that this expression goes back to the English playwright John Dennis (1657–1734), who had constructed a "thunder-making device" around 1700 and been vexed that it was stolen by his rivals. That's possible, but the Italians were stealing "thunder" a century before the English dramatist was born. In sixteenth-century Italy *tuono* ("thunder") was a slang term for "cannon." In the intensely competitive atmosphere of Italian warmaking, it was not unknown for the commander of one *battaglione* to "borrow" the artillery of another commander on the same side. This practice led to the expressions *tuono prestare* ("borrow thunder") and *tuone rubare* ("steal thunder"), first as descriptions of the practices themselves, and then as descriptions of situations in which one person's property, or precedence, or *onore*, had been peremptorily "set aside" by another.

Vitelloni (see vittles) made much of this practice as an opportunity for taking offense. His recommendation for reprisal was a sensible one: Steal the thief's firebrands, so he will have nothing with which to touch off the cannon. In England, thanks to Foxpaw's translation, this practice became "stealing a match" and eventually, through mispronunciation, *stealing a march*.

Tie One On

This translates a Romanche expression, *se liar su*, meaning "to tie *oneself* on." In Romanche-speaking Switzerland, this is something you do *after* you have drunk too much: It does not refer to the drinking itself, but to mountaineers' safety ropes. The Swiss typically use these ropes not only when they are scaling Alpine peaks but also when two people are returning from a tavern late at night, and one is too unsteady to negotiate the mountain trails without assistance. In these situations, the drunken friend ties himself onto his more surefooted companion. In urban America, where many Swiss settled in the last century, the original meaning was lost, and the *one*—which had once meant the actor—became misapplied to the act.

Give a Toast

In England beginning about the fifteenth century, it was fashionable to serve toast with mulled wine: The bread was dipped in the liquid and then eaten, much as we do with donuts and coffee. Around 1525, Henry VIII's official chef, a Frenchman named Geryon, came up with a twist on the custom. Using a very fine butter brush, he would paint diners' initials and even short messages on the bread before toasting it, so that it would brown differentially, and the king's guests might have personalized snacks. The idea was enormously popular with Henry's courtiers, who began to suggest messages to Geryon which they could then present, on the toast, to the king. Thus "toasting" served the purposes of court sycophancy, not to mention the monarch's prodigious appetite. Eventually those who had ordered the toasts began to read the messages aloud rather than presenting the physical morsels themselves; these verbal "toast plaudits" were the prototype of our drinking *toasts* today.

Every Tom, Dick, and Harry

There was an original Tom, an original Dick, and an original Harry—although none of them was terribly original. Collectively they were known as the Rimington Valley Rhymaires, a turn-of-the-century vaudeville act that seems to have been an embarrassment even to the audiences on its own upstate New York circuit. Booked into a Brooklyn, New York, theater in 1908 by a promoter with more courage than common sense, the trio succeeded only in putting most of the audience to sleep with its highly derivative singing and dancing, and in eliciting this snappish comment from a reviewer: "They are the very definition of the banal. They are oatmeal without the raisins. They are ministers plenipotentiary from the international court of Lord Bland." They closed after one night, leaving us with the phrase *every Tom, Dick, and Harry* to signify the absence of individual style. It is hardly surprising that no one recorded their last names.

Tongue in Cheek

The first person to use the expression *tongue in cheek* to mean insincere or facetious was Girolamo Vitelloni (see VITTLES). Vitelloni recommended the actual placement of the tongue in one's cheek as part of a *gesto offensivo*, or insult gesture, that was meant to accompany false praise. The idea was for the person wishing to give offense to compliment his target publicly and profusely, and then to make a visible bulge in his cheek with his tongue, as a signal to onlookers that he had just told a lie. The iconographic explanation of the gesture seemed to be that the speaker was stifling a laugh, although Yarrowville presents an alternate rationale that is both entertainable and entertaining: The bulging cheek gesture, he suggests, made it appear as if the speaker had a mouthful of water that he was about to spit on the person being addressed. Whatever the "deep function" of the gesture, it became popular throughout Europe in the sixteenth century as a broad way of showing insincerity. The English were especially fond of the practice. It is no accident that their term *cheeky*, meaning brazenly impudent, became current at the same time: to *show cheek,* in Elizabethan times, meant to display Vitelloni's famous gesture.

Carry a Torch

To *carry a torch* for someone is to love that person in spite of rejection. The phrase, and an accompanying custom, originated in Greece, where spurned lovers would stand beneath their beloveds' balconies and plead for their favors by the light of torches. The modern expression *torch singer*, for a specialist in plaintive nightclub tunes, actually goes back to the ancient world; the Homeric phrase (applied to Penelope's suitors) is *dada psallos*, literally, "singer with a torch."

A modern aside: Note that English *torch* is Greek *dada*. Art historians commonly suggest that the Dadaist movement of the 1910s took its name from the French term *dada*, for "hobby horse." This idea was a Dadaist RED HERRING. It is no accident that Marcel Duchamp, father of the Dadaists, began his career as a classics professor. His memoirs have made perfectly clear that the origin of the term was the Greek for *torch*. And this makes far more sense than the "hobby horse" explanation, for the Dadaists were nothing if not incendiary: They wanted to "torch" artistic tradition.

Down the Tubes

The tubes referred to here are a submarine's torpedo tubes. In both world wars, those cylinders projected into the water not just their usual lethal cargo, but also day-to-day garbage and, in emergency situations, bits of debris designed to convince a surface attacker that the sub had been sunk. Hence *down the tubes* as a description for anything useless or lost.

Ugly as Sin

Christians have often used this metaphor to emphasize the unattractiveness of vice. But the expression predates Christianity by about 2,000 years. Shinn was an Ugaritic river god with an unquenchable thirst for human blood and a face, as the Ugaritic adage had it, "that could stop a sun dial." Many of the peoples of the Middle East, who at one time or another had come under the influence of the expansionist empire of Ugarit, incorporated the Ugaritic expression *yecch-shinn* into their own vernaculars, and it was because of this diffusion that "ugly as Shinn" entered first Jewish, and then Christian, slang. There is even some speculation, particularly by Professor Mia Culpa of the University of No Return, that when Jesus spoke of death as the wages of sin, he really meant the wages of Shinn: the human sacrifices that the Ugarites offered to the deity to keep him from wholesale depradations.

Uh-Huh/Uhn-Uh

Uh-huh for "yes" and *uhn-uh* for "no" may seem like arbitrary grunts, but they are not. They were devised in 1777 by Benjamin Franklin, who had made a study of English and American phonetics and had concluded that these two nonsense sounds might serve the patriot cause, as he told the Continental Congress, "in the same manner that the shibboleth had served the Gileadites." The Gileadites in the Book of Judges had discovered a number of Ephraimite spies by asking them to pronounce the word *shib-*

boleth, which means both "ear of wheat" and "stream of water." The *sh* sound being absent from the Ephraimite phonetic system, they could only utter "sibboleth," and so "forty and two thousand" of them were put to death. It was Franklin's inspiration to use *uh-huh* and *uhn-uh* as alternate passwords in American encampments, reasoning that British spies, even if they did manage to get the right password on a given day, would still have so much trouble mastering the subtle distinction that they would easily be discovered.

Congress thought enough of Franklin's scheme to recommend it to George Washington, and that is where the idea fell apart. The general himself, it was discovered, could not distinguish between the two passwords, and this meant that, had they been adopted, he himself might have been hung as a traitor. Recent computer research into the Washington family neural history, conducted by the Smithsonian Institution's Bea Nudles, has revealed that Washington suffered from aphasia, or an impairment of the power to utter words. Nudles suggests, quite sanely, that this could account not only for his bad showing on Franklin's test, but also his celebrated inability to tell a lie.

Vittles

Girolamo Vitelloni was an eccentric Italian nobleman whose sole written work, *Il Manuale Maschio*, satirized Renaissance "courtesy books" by presenting detailed instructions for breaches of etiquette. Published in 1532, the book was specifically an attack on the idea of the Renaissance gentleman as presented in Castiglione's *Book of the Courtier*. Like that small classic, it was quickly spread through Europe in translations; the first English translation was William Foxpaw's 1537 version, *The True Man's Vade Mecum, or The Manly Arte of Giving Offense*.

Vitelloni outlined three distinct categories of *offessia maschio*, or "manly offense." The first was *verbo offensivo*, or verbal insult (an idea of his instructions for this type is suggested in the entries FUDDY-DUDDY and HANKY-PANKY). The second category was *gesto offensivo*, or the offensive gesture (for examples of this type, see BACK OF ONE'S HAND, LAUGHING UP ONE'S SLEEVE, and TONGUE IN CHEEK). The final, and most inventive, category was that of the *atto offensivo*, or offensive act, and it is because of his championship of this type of insult that Vitelloni is remembered in the word *vittles*.

Vittles today means simply "food." In sixteenth-century Europe, thanks to the *Manuale Maschio*, it meant a very special kind of food: small, often partially chewed table scraps. On Vitelloni's recommendation, if you wished to insult a rival publicly, one of the most effective methods of doing so was to strew refuse of this sort in front of his house, as if to imply that he was no better than a dog. The practice enjoyed a vogue in England in the 1540s, and the scraps themselves became known as *vitellonis*, then *vittles*.

One kind of *vittle* was particularly offensive. If you could manage to place small, just-roasted potatoes at the person's gate, you were implying, in Foxpaw's delicate translation, "that his potatoes, that is to saye his tessticals, bee full of more ardor than capabilitie." It is from this curious practice that we get the expressions *hot potato*, meaning something that you wish to get rid of; and *small potatoes,* meaning something of little or no consequence.

It is not clear whether Vitelloni was a truly cantankerous soul who meant his book itself as an *atto offensivo*, or whether he intended it good-naturedly, to prick the pretensions of the time. In any event, the joke was better received abroad than in this odd writer's native Urbino. The powerful Duke of Urbino, who had supported Castiglione enthusiastically, had Vitelloni exiled in 1536, as an "*atto deffensivo* of public morals." Vitelloni went, evidently, to England, where he assisted in Foxpaw's translation and helped to popularize not only the expressions indicated here, but also your NAME IS MUD.

Wacky

Wacky is World War II slang for "crazy." Originally it was a be-mused but rather affectionate army term, applied to members of the Women's Army Corps, or WACs. The idea here went beyond the conventional male delusion that all women are a little bit cracked and therefore incomprehensible; the WACs were thought to be especially hard to understand because they had volunteered for service in a man's world. Gradually, as the term acquired the more general connotation of "odd" or "unbalanced," it was ap-plied to male soldiers as well, particularly to those suffering battle fatigue.

On/Off the Wagon

American temperance societies a hundred years ago were more brazen and influential than they are today. Especially in rural areas, the weekly temperance lecture, sponsored by church and civic groups, was as much a regular feature of 1880s life as labor agitation or fringe-top surreys. But that was the least of the rum-haters' weapons. The full-scale march or parade, with tambou-rines and bugles and much bottle-smashing, was a much more popular method of gaining converts, and often a highlight of such parades was a kind of rolling theater called the Water Wagon. This was usually a local farmer's borrowed buckboard on which reformers and those they had rescued from the gutter would enact tableaux and even short plays illustrating the dangers of drink. The wagon might be divided into two "rooms," for example, with one showing the sodden coarseness of a drinker and the other showing him spruced up and saved. Or a local imbiber, recently reformed, might give testimony from the wagon about his cure, all the while dipping gleefully into a water bucket and showering the crowd with the curative liquid. For a town drunk to be "on the Water Wagon," then, meant he was the show of that day. To be *off the wagon*—or worse, to have fallen *off the wagon*—meant you had backslid into old ways.

The social appeal of the Water Wagon—part theater and part religion—is documented ably in Grant Wiggins's history, *Out of Their Cups: The Temperance Giants.* A particularly useful feature of this book is the appendix of period drinking (and antidrinking) songs, including the Reverend Mace Butler's rousing "I'd Rather Be Sober Than President" and the anonymous, plaintive ballad "Falling Off the Wagon Again."

Off the Wall

This expression originated in southern France where, beginning in the seventeenth century, restaurants wrote their menus of the day on a slate-covered wall near the kitchen—the precursor of the modern blackboard menu. In establishments where special, nonmenu orders were taken, these were known as *plats au loin du mur*, or "dishes off the wall." Montcalm's soldiers brought the expression to North America during the French and Indian Wars, and here it began to be applied to strange people and ideas as well as food. Hence the current connotation of "unconventional" or "bizarre."

Waltz Right In

Why should "waltzing" into a room or situation carry the negative connotation of reckless intrusion? Because the first Europeans to waltz were the Poles, that much abused nation of romantics who were being considered intruders by the Germans centuries before the American Polish joke was born. The German verb *walzen* means "to roll," and the fluid Polish dance was called the waltz because it looked, to the geometric Nordic mind, like aimless "rolling." Thus for a nondancing person to "waltz," in German as later in English, was for him to behave like a Pole:

to come across with gross bonhomie and easy rhythms, with not a thought for good Germanic form. The Poles, incidentally, have a response—actually, two responses. Kraków slang for "German" is *sztyvnobiodrowi*, or "the rigid-hipped ones." And throughout Czechoslovakia and Hungary as well as Poland, the worst insult you can give to a dancing partner is to say that he dances like a German.

Wet Behind the Ears

This expression, indicating inexperience or simply youth, comes from the quite sensible practice of toweling off a newborn baby's head and body to remove blood and amniotic fluid. The mouth and nose are cleared of fluid first, to prevent suffocation, and such noncritical areas as the spaces behind the ears and between the fingers and the toes are done last. The younger the newborn, therefore, the wetter behind the ears. The wetter the toes and fingers too, of course—so it is not surprising that in medieval France many artisan guilds referred to their youngest apprentices as *enfants des doigts humides*, or "the Wet-Finger Kids." (Contrary to popular opinion, this expression did not refer to the supposed clumsiness of apprentices.)

Wet Blanket

In the early days of the far western fur trade, the Indians of the plains and mountains found that their traditional method of communicating long distance by smoke signal profitted by the replacement of their time-honored smoke-control tool, the animal skin, with the white man's lighter and less flammable woolen blanket. But even blankets could catch fire, and so signalers would keep them slightly damp. If the blankets were too damp, of course, they could extinguish the signal fire; hence the Shoshonean adage "He rains on the blanket and cannot speak," which illustrates the hazard of using too much water. Mountain men, adopting the signaling procedure and the proverb, gave us the expression *wet blanket* to describe a person who inhibits conversation and enjoyment by his "dampening" behavior.

Wheel and Deal

This phrase reflects the aura of suspicion that has always surrounded entrepreneurial activity. From the late Middle Ages on, *to wheel* meant to play a wheel of fortune, such as roulette, at a public fair or private gaming house; *to deal* meant to deal, and bet, at cards. So to *wheel and deal* at business meant to link your commercial success to such unsavory, not to mention unChristian, activities as acquisitiveness, wagering, and "fixed" games. Grose's *Dictionary of the Vulgar Tongue* gives a notice of the phrase in 1525, appropriately at the beginning of the commercial Renaissance. The related phrase *big wheel* he tracks down to 1541, when it meant "one who wins big on the wheel." Compare the modern American carnival expression *eighteen-wheeler*, which means someone who wins big at roulette by landing on "lucky eighteen."

Smart as a Whip

In British as in American usage, a whip is a member of a political party appointed to "whip up" support for party platforms by over-seeing the discipline of its members. Specifically, the whip sees to it that legislators get to important voting sessions on time, and that they vote right when they do get there. The term dates from the early nineteenth century, when the many pleasures of a grow-ing London provided ample distractions to lazy legislators, and when consequently the absentee rate was running high. Because of the number of possible nonparliamentarian "engagements"— London in the 1830s had literally hundreds of gaming houses, ale houses, and brothels—party whips had to be ingenious in order to track down missing members, and the expression *smart as a whip* reflects that fact: It arose as grudging praise for their diligence. Lord Jeffrey Mimsy-Malmsey, who sat for Leicester from 1832 to 1837, confessed in his memoirs that the whips of that era were "deucedly smart": "One of them—was it that young chap Peel? I can't recall—ferreted me down from out in Bat-tersea—Battersea, mind you—and would not even let me buy my round before spiriting me back to the House floor. I could never show my face in Battersea again. And what came of it but that stupid Reform Bill?"

Whole Nine Yards

In traditional India a *nabob*, or provincial administrator, was issued a silk sash denoting rank. The length of the sash varied, with short, cummerbund-style sashes being given to the lowest-level factotums and progressively longer sashes being issued to their hierarchical superiors. Nineteenth-century British gover-nors, ever with an eye out for precision, got the idea of measuring these badges of office to clarify the native administrative structure, and they subsequently put rations on silk fabric, since the material was in demand back in England. Before the British came, nabob sashes could measure as long as twenty or thirty yards, giving the highest administrators a bulky appearance that led to the Anglo-Indian insult *tub of guts* to describe a royal governor. The British cut the limit back to nine yards and allowed this ration only to the highest officials. Thus to go, or to get, *the whole nine yards* was to excel in achievement or status. (For more on *nabobs*, see SWANK.)

The Willies

To get (or have) the *willies* means to feel unaccountably nervous, or "jittery." The figure of speech comes from Louisiana, where in folk belief a *volee* is a spirit of the dead. The name comes from the French verb *voler*, which means both "to fly" and "to steal." The *volees*, according to a combined Creole and Cajun tradition, are the ghosts of people who have died after falling, or being pushed, from high places. Typically, they haunt aviaries and poultry markets, stealing feathers to make themselves wings so that when they return to earth at the Second Coming they will not suffer the same fate again. Many Louisiana bayou folk, whenever they cook a *poulet au pot*, set one wing outside the door for these creatures so they will not be disturbed by them at dinner. When Cajun people hear noises or experience inexplicable "goings on" at night—such as furniture being moved or doors being opened—they say that "the house has the *volees*." It was the English translation of this phrase—in French, *la maison á les volees*—that gave us *the willies*. Broadening in meaning as it traveled upriver, *the willies* came to mean not just apprehensiveness about ghosts but uneasiness in general.

Willy-Nilly

As the *Oxford English Dictionary* makes clear, the original meaning of this term was "without choice" or "under compulsion"; it described something that would happen "will he or nil he," that is, whether or not a concerned party wished it to. In modern times, however, it frequently means "disorganized" or "haphazard," and the likeliest explanation for this accretion is to be found in Australia. There, in the 1890s, *willy-willy* was bush slang for a hurricane, and Willy and Nell were a popular vaudeville team whose offerings favored slapstick and non sequiturs. Since *willy-nilly* first took on its current sense about this time, we can suspect a vernacular fusion, evoking both the disorder wrought by a hurricane and the verbally reckless style of the comic duo. The theater writer for the Willoughby *Evening Post*, one Nelson Will, suggested as much in his 1897 review of the vaudeville act. "Willy and Nell forced this Nel Will, *willy-nilly*, into hysterics. They are a very willy willy of nelly nonsense. Should you ask whether, willy or nilly, they will have a long run, this Will would say, *willy-nilly*, that they will." Will, as you might surmise from *his* "nelly nonsense," was a palindromist on the side.

Winging It

There is no mystery about this term. In the MADCAP days of early aviation, when aircraft engines were far less reliable than they are now, many pilots had to set their birds down after the motors had conked out; since the only stability available in this type of powerless landing came from the deft manipulation of the ailerons, it was only "wings and wit," in flyer jargon, that could save your skin. Hence *winging it* for any impromptu and resourceful endeavor.

Wishy-Washy

This is an old prospecting terms dating from the California Gold Rush. In panning for gold, you place river bottom into a large metal pan, swish it around with water, and hope that, when the gravel and silt sloshes over the side, you are left with a quantity of (heavier) gold. A pan that *pans out* or *washes* contains gold; one that *doesn't wash* comes up empty. *Wishy-washy* was a compromise term: It was used to describe a stretch of river where the amount and quality of gold was so low that you needed prodigious amounts of energy—and not a little wishful thinking—to extract it. On a *wishy-washy* claim, veteran prospector Fred C. Dobbs explained in his memoir *Getting the Goods*, "You'd spend twelve hours washing, twelve hours wishing, and another three hours a day wondering why." Hence *wishy-washy* came to describe anything—from a gold claim to an expression of opinion—that lacked the desired conviction or "fortitude."

The Works

The *works*, meaning everything (as on a hamburger or pizza) is English shorthand for the French term *chefs d'oeuvre*. Usually translated as "masterpiece," *chef d'oeuvre* actually means "master of the work." If French were as rational a language as the Académie Française would like us to believe, the expression would read *oeuvre du chef*, or "work of the master," since it is clearly the work, and not its maker, that is substantive when we speak of a "master's piece." Things get even worse when we come to the plural. *Chefs d'oeuvre* should mean the (plural) masters of a (single) work, but in everyday usage it means the (single) master's (plural) works. It is these plural *works* that the modern master, or chef, places on top of a pizza.

Set the World on Fire

According to legend, when Alexander the Great was a youth, the gods offered him the choice of a long and uneventful life or a short and glorious one. Being a Macedonian, he chose the latter, and it is because of his choice that we have the phrase *set the world on fire.* Alexander succeeded to the Macedonian throne in 336 B.C., when he was not yet twenty-one. For the next thirteen years, he cut a swath of fire and blood from Greece all the way to the Indus, creating an empire that stunned his contemporaries and that made him seem, even while he was alive, a practically supernatural being. When he died in 323 B.C. at the age of thirty-three, he had acquired a skein of epithets that testified to his military prowess: "The Great" was of course the most common, but in reference to his treatment of captured cities, he was also called "the Leveler" and "the Tower Burner." This latter epithet reflected the fact that, in an almost literal sense, his armies had put the entire world to the torch.

In the Middle Ages, when romances based on Alexander's exploits provided the "good reads" of the day, the Latin expressions *turrem incendere* ("to burn a tower") and *mundum incendere* ("to burn the world") became vernacular descriptions for great achievements, especially those of an expansive, public nature. At the same time, the self-deprecating admission that you didn't *want* to torch towers (or towns) became a formulaic claim to humility; it was a way of providing a good, Christian distance between yourself and the ancient pagan conqueror.

That's a Wrap

When a filmmaker is satisfied with a scene, he may announce *"That's a wrap"*—meaning no more "takes" need be made, and the actors may "wrap it up" for the day. This genial bit of shoptalk reflects a matter of some gravity from the Silent Era. In those days, when film was made of highly volatile celluloid and when backup prints were often beyond budget, a film company's greatest fear was a stockroom fire, since it could wipe out the hard work of months. To protect the film from combustion, it was placed within a paraffin-sealed can and the can was then wrapped in damp cloths. So to "wrap it up" in the early days had a serious, and quite literal, meaning.

Wrong Side of the Bed

The Opium Wars which Queen Victoria's armies waged against China in 1839 and 1858 were fought principally to determine whether or not the civilized English had the right to impose drug addiction on the barbarian Chinese. The Treaty of Tientsin (1858) established that right, and also opened China up to foreign penetration. By the treaty terms, all Chinese ports were opened to trade, missionaries were allowed into the interior, and foreigners were permitted for the first time to navigate the Yangtze River. This last stipulation led to a series of humorous incidents that gave us the expression "getting up on the *wrong side of the bed*."

In the 1850s, as now, many Chinese lived on river houseboats, and during the summer months it was common for houseboat dwellers to sleep not in the stifling hold, but out on deck. When British soldiers stationed on the Yangtze adopted this practice, Chinese youths chafing at the burdens of peace introduced a guerilla tactic designed to embarrass the foreigners they could not defeat. Swimming up to an anchored British houseboat in the dead of night, they would reach silently over the gunwale, pull a sleeping soldier over the side, and escape while he thrashed in the water. No drownings were reported, but the injured pride of the victims naturally caused them to be peevish in the morning, and that was enough to give rise to predictable kidding by comrades. The jocular, formulaic observation "You get up on the *wrong side of the bed*?" soon passed into the language as a response to any sullenness or pique.

Catch Some Zs

The Zs referred to in this pithy metaphor for sleep are the zigzag teeth of a handsaw. A traditional English folk remedy for insomnia was to do heavy manual labor before retiring, and "catching the Zs"—that is, making the saw teeth "catch" in the wood—was considered particularly effective in this regard. Thus the expression referred originally not to the act of sleeping itself, but to the work that would make that act possible. Cartoonists who depict a sleeping person dreaming about sawing wood are also referring to this practice.

The idea that the *z* sound is related to snoring has been suggested by many writers, but is without phonemic evidence. Recent studies of snoring patterns done by Professor R. E. M. Yawn, in fact, show that the wavelength profile of the most common North American snore is closest in configuration to that of a uvular. This has led him, in the latest *Somnological Journal*, to offer the neologistic phrase "catch some Rs" as more accurate, and to call for an end to the "tyranny of Z."

Bibliography

Sources for individual entries are identified in the text by author and title. The following volumes, referred to only by authors' names, were more generally helpful:

Culdesack
Dwayne Culdesack & Deedee Culdesack, *Why We Talk So Good: Origins of Catchy Phrases*, 1931.

Fetch & Tarry
Beatrice Fetch & Morris Tarry, *Dumb, Drunk & Daffy: A Dictionary of Terms Relating to Incompetence*, 1975.

Frogg
Maurice Frogg, *A Franglais Handbook*, 1967.

Ronald & Peck
J. F. Ronald & Yancey Peck, *A Dictionary of American Idia on Hysterical Principles*, 19th ed., 1986.

Seagull
Erika Livingston Seagull, *Getting Rich Off Latin: A User's Guide*, 1972.

Squab
Bennett Squab, *What Partridge Left Out: A Dictionary of Even Less Conventional English*, 3rd ed., 1985.

Tschako
T. F. T. A. Tschako, *"Deutsch Marks" in English*, 1959.

Yarrowville
Alexander Yarrowville, M.A., *Cockney and Other English Street Slang*, 1897.

Index

About the Author

Born in New Brunswick, NJ, in 1944, Tad Tuleja is a graduate of Yale, Cornell, and the University of Sussex. He's been a columnist, editor, educator, ghostwriter, novelist, and researcher, as well as an author (or coauthor) of books on pop psychology, coupon-clipping, diamond investment, business ethics, and selling—and a series of short-entry reference books. His twenty-three published works include *Land of Precious Snow*, a novel, as well as *Strategic Selling, Beyond the Bottom Line*, *Fabulous Fallacies*, *Namesakes*, *Curious Customs*, and three adventure novels written under the nom de mayhem Marshall Macao. Tuleja lives with his wife and three children in Belchertown, Massachusetts.